Leonard Allison Morrison

Historical

The earliest history and genealogy, covering nearly three hundred years,

from about 1600 to 1891, of the Dinsmoor-Dinsmore family of Scotland,

Ireland, and America

Leonard Allison Morrison

Historical
The earliest history and genealogy, covering nearly three hundred years, from about 1600 to 1891, of the Dinsmoor-Dinsmore family of Scotland, Ireland, and America

ISBN/EAN: 9783337323288

Printed in Europe, USA, Canada, Australia, Japan

Cover: Foto ©ninafisch / pixelio.de

More available books at **www.hansebooks.com**

THE EARLIEST HISTORY AND GENEALOGY,

COVERING NEARLY THREE HUNDRED YEARS, FROM
ABOUT 1600 TO 1891, OF THE

DINSMOOR-DINSMORE FAMILY

OF SCOTLAND, IRELAND, AND AMERICA;

WITH THAT OF MANY OF THEIR DESCENDANTS, AND
ADDITIONAL FACTS RELATING TO THE SIXTEEN
FIRST SETTLERS AND THEIR FAMILIES OF
LONDONDERRY, NEW HAMPSHIRE,
WHO EMIGRATED TO AMERICA
IN 1719;

Also, Statistics Concerning the McKean and Bell Families;

WITH A POEM, "THE HEROES OF THE SIEGE OF
LONDONDERRY, IRELAND, 1688-89."

By LEONARD ALLISON MORRISON, A. M.,

OF WINDHAM, NEW HAMPSHIRE.

—————

LOWELL, MASS.
MORNING MAIL PRINT: No. 147 CENTRAL STREET.
1891.

Leonard A. Morrison

THE DINSMOOR FAMILY.

This family of historic fame is of Scotch blood, and in the earliest account of any of this race their home is found upon Scottish soil.

ORIGIN OF THE NAME.

The name Dinsmoor is rarely found in Scotland, although Dunsmore is frequently seen, and Dinsmuir and Dinsmore are occasionally observed. In Ireland, the patronymic is borne by many persons in the vicinity of Ballymoney, County Antrim, and they are presumably descendants of John Dinsmoor[2], the emigrant to Ulster from Scotland. Dinsmoor appears as the original method of spelling, and was generally followed till about 1800. Since then it became the fashion for some to spell their name Dinsmore, and it is frequently seen as Dunsmoor, Dunmore, Dunsmore, Densmore, Densmoor, but generally the orthography is Dinsmoor and Dinsmore, the latter methods frequently appearing in the same family, and often each has been adopted by the same individual at different periods of life.

The family is not an ancient one, nor, on the whole, very numerous; and upon the other side of the water the name has never been borne, to my knowledge, by the gentry or nobility. The Dinsmoors were commoners. Rev. John W. Dinsmore, D. D., of Bloomington, Ill., gives this as the probable origin of this patronymic: —

"I have no doubt but that the original ancestor wrote, if he could write, Dunsemoor (*dunse*, a little hill, and *moor*, heath). He probably lived on, or by, a little hill at the edge of the heath, or moor."

THE FIRST KNOWN DINSMOOR.

1. *Laird* Dinsmoor[1], the progenitor, and earliest known ancestor of the Dinsmoors, was a Scotchman, born in Auld Scotia certainly not far from the year 1600. The fact that he was called *Laird* would indicate that he was a man of some note and consequence in his locality. He was a farmer, had tenants under him and dwelt on the bank of the flowing Tweed, at a place which tradition has variously called Achenmead, Auchinmede, Aikenmead, and other variations of the name. This spot has not been identified and located by his inquiring and investigating descendants. Tradition asserts that he was a follower and adherent of Douglass, and as one of those powerful chiefs had his home in a fortress whose walls were of wondrous thickness and strength, placed on a projecting rock in a fiercely wind-swept and narrow defile, on the north bank of the River Tweed, known as Neidpath Castle, near the City of Peebles, it is not amiss to hazard the conjecture that *Laird* Dinsmoor's home was in the immediate vicinity. Fair and beautiful is that locality, and the river, as it rushes through the deep gorge on its way from the highlands to the sea, sings of Scotland, and is itself one of the fairest streams in the home of our forefathers.

Of the mental characteristics of the *Laird* we know but little. But it is evident that he was strongly imbued with the prevailing principle of his age, that the eldest born should receive undue homage and respect from the younger, — a sentiment which was repugnant to the second son, to his American descendants, and to all Americans. His home being upon the bank of the Tweed, as he was living there some two hundred and twenty-five years ago, or about 1667, it is probable that he finished his days in the land of his birth, and that his dust mingles with the soil of his native Scotland.

"Requiescat in pace."

CHILDREN OF LAIRD DINSMOOR[1], OF SCOTLAND.

2. —— Dinsmoor[2], whose Christian name is not known, was born in Scotland, presumably about 1648. He remained in Scotland, and being the *eldest*, inherited his father's titles, dignities, homage, and respect.

3. John Dinsmoor[2], of Ballywattick, Ballymoney, Ireland.

John Dinsmoor[2], b. in Scotland, presumably about 1650. He was required, by his father, it is said, with uncovered head, to hold the off stirrup of his elder brother's saddle, when he mounted his horse. He felt humiliated by the requirement, and in his seventeenth year, or about 1667, he forsook his father's house and early home, his kindred and native land, and went forth, bearing no property or goods with him, save a cane in his hand, his wearing apparel upon his person, with striped woollen hose upon his stalwart feet, and a gray bonnet of huge extent which covered his independent and manly head. Thus he left his native land, and thus he first appeared in the Province of Ulster, in the Parish of Ballywattick, one of the town lands of Ballymoney, County of Antrim, Ireland. For, like thousands of others of the best blood of the Lowlands of Scotland at that time, he crossed the belt of sea dividing the two countries, and helped to reclaim the cruelly confiscated land of the native Celts. There he made his home, and although the young adventurer was in a foreign land, yet he was surrounded, not by a strange people, but by those of his own race and nation. He was married, at the age of twenty, about 1670, was left a widower at seventy, lived a widower for twenty-nine years, and was "gathered to his fathers" at the great age of ninety-nine years. He was widely known for his good sense, his moral worth, his fervent piety.

He established the home in Ballywattick, and for generations his descendants have there resided, the last of them leaving the place in 1838.

CHILDREN OF JOHN DINSMOOR[2], THE SCOTCH EMIGRANT TO IRELAND.

4. John Dinsmoor[3] (see No. 8), b. as early as 1671, in Ballywattick, Ballymoney, County Antrim, Ireland. Emigrated to Londonderry, N. H., that portion which is now Windham, N. H., as early as 1723, and is the ancestor of most of the Dinsmoors of New Hampshire.
5. Robert Dinsmoor[3] (12), b. in Ballywattick, Ireland, as early as 1673; res. Ballywattick, Ireland; living there in 1715.
6. Adam Dinsmoor[3] (58), b. Ballywattick as early as 1675; of him there is extant no exact record, only the general one, that he lived at Ballywattick, Ireland, was the ancestor of many Dinsmoors, and has had his name perpetuated in his descendants and distant relatives in succeeding generations to the present time.
7. Samuel Dinsmoor[3], b. Ballywattick, Ireland, presumably as early as 1677; of him there is no definite record. But we know that these three brothers, Adam[3], Robert[3], and Samuel[3], were the ancestors of most, if not all, of the Dinsmoors now in Ireland, and of those

who have emigrated from Ireland to the United States at diffe
times, with the exception of John Dinsmoor', their brothe
New Hampshire, and his descendants.

8. John Dinsmoor' (4), John[2], *Laird* Dinsmoor'.
was b. in Ballywattick, Ballymoney, County Antrim,
land, as early as 1671 (as his son Robert was b. in 169
was the progenitor of most of the Dinsmoors of Ne
Hampshire, and came to America as early as 1723. He
was taken prisoner by the Indians, and, after vari s
adventures, finally made his appearance in the Scotch t-
tlement of Londonderry, N. H. With many of the peo
there he was acquainted, having known them in Ireland.
He made his home in what is now Windham. Being a
mason, he built a stone house, in which he lived, and
where he d. in 1741. The place is occupied, in 1891, by
Phineas D. Scott. His wife and children joined him i
Windham, N. H.

CHILDREN, BORN IN BALLYWATTICK, IRELAND.

9. Robert Dinsmoor[4] 11, b. 1692; res. Windham, N. H.
10. Elizabeth Dinsmoor[4], m. John Hopkins, lived near her father . e
brother in Windham, N. H., and was the ancestor of most of
Hopkins name in that section of the country.

11. Robert Dinsmoor[4] (9), previously mentione .
m. Margaret Orr. in Ireland, and he and his wife a i
four children came to New Hampshire in 1730. He w
prominent in the town, filled various public positions,
and his last years were spent upon the farm owned in
1891 by Edwin O. Dinsmoor, a descendant, four gene
tions removed. He d. Oct. 14, 1751. His wife d. June
2, 1752.

Many of their descendants have risen to distinction,
and high honors have crowned the labors of their lives,
among them Col. Silas Dinsmoor[6] (John[5], Robert[4],
John[3], John[2], *Laird* Dinsmoor[1]), his grandson, th
noted Indian agent, a man of versatility of gifts, c
marked ability, who was b. in Windham, N. H., Sept
26, 1766, and d. at Bellevue, Ky., June 17, 1847. I s
wife was Mary Gordon, and his son, Thomas A.
Dinsmoor[7], lives at Kirksville, Adair Co., Mo. Rob
Dinsmoor[4] (William[5], Robert[4], John[3], John[2], *La*
Dinsmoor[1]), his grandson, was well known as the "R
tic Bard," a volume of whose poems, mostly written

the Scotch, dialect was published. He was b. in Windham, Oct. 7, 1757, and d. there March 16, 1836. A brother of the latter was Gov. Samuel Dinsmoor[6], b. in Windham, N. H., July 1, 1766, a graduate of Dartmouth College, a member of Congress, and Governor of New Hampshire. He m. Mary Boyd Reid, daughter of General Reid of Revolutionary fame, and d. March 15, 1835. Their son, Samuel Dinsmoor[7], was also Governor of New Hampshire. They lived in Keene, N. H. Margaret Dinsmoor[6], a sister of the "Rustic Bard" and of the elder Governor, was b. Oct. 15, 1759; m. Dea. Samuel Morison, and d. in Windham, Sept. 18, 1837. Their son, Jeremiah Morrison[7], b. April 20, 1795, d. Nov. 24, 1862; m. Eleanor Reed Kimball, and were the parents of Hon. Leonard Allison Morrison[8], eighth generation from *Laird* Dinsmoor[1], of Scotland. He was b. in Windham, N. H., Feb. 21, 1843, resides there, has been a member of the House and Senate of the New Hampshire Legislature, and is the author of this book. Two great-grandsons of Robert Dinsmoor[4], (John[3], John[2], *Laird* Dinsmoor[1]), by his son John[5], John[6], were James Dinsmoor[7], of Boone County, Ky., a man of ability, and his brother, John Bell Dinsmoor[7], of Ripley, N. Y. Rev. Cadford M. Dinsmoor[8], of Exeter, N. H., son of John Taylor Gilman Dinsmoor[7] (James[6], Robert[5], Robert[4], John[3], John[2], *Laird* Dinsmoor[1]), a Methodist clergyman, was b. in Windham, N. H., Aug. 20, 1826; graduated at Wesleyan University in 1851. Hon. James Dinsmoor[7], of Sterling, Ill. (William[6], William[5], Robert[4], John[3], John[2], *Laird* Dinsmoor[1], of Scotland.) He was b. in Windham, N. H, March 3, 1818; graduated at Dartmouth College in 1841; is a lawyer of high standing, resided in Lowell, Mass., and was a member of the Massachusetts House of Representatives. Removed to Sterling, Ill., in 1856, and for four years was a member of the Illinois Legislature. He is the author of the History of the Dinsmoor Family, 75 pp., embodied in the "History of Windham in New Hampshire." It is one of the most valuable family histories extant, and is a monument to the great industry and love of kindred possessed by its honored author. He m. Amanda A. Carpenter, of Sharon, Vt., who d. Aug. 14, 1886; in the following year, June 1, 1887, he m., 2d, her sister, Mrs. Ma y M (Carpenter) True. His son, Jarvis Dinsmoor[9], is a law yer in Sterling, Ill., and two daughters who gradua ed at Vassar College — Abee Dinsmoor[9], a teacher; Fl rence Amanda Dinsmoor[9], m. James F. Covey, res. St ling, Ill. Hon. Albert E. Pillsbury[9], a brilliant lawye and attorney general of the State of Massachusetts, s of Dinsmoor blood, as his mother, Elizabeth Dinsmo [7], is a sister of Hon. James Dinsmoor[7], lawyer and a hor. She m. Joseph Webster Pillsbury, and resides in M d, N. H. The list of prominent descendants of the w Hampshire emigrant would not be complete w   t mention being made of William B. Dinsmore[7], Es ., late president of the Adams Express Company, the arg est express company in the word. (He was son of Will iam[6], John[5], Robert[4], John[3], John[2], *Laird* Dinsm r[1] of distant Achenmead, Scotland.) He was b. in s ter, Mass., July, 1810, and d. April 13, 1888; 1 m. Augusta M. Snow, of Brewster, Mass. He poss d marvellous powers for business, a massive mind and y pic, and an inexhaustible fund of wit and hu r. He r sided at Staatsburg, N. Y., and is succeeded 1 i sons, William B. Dinsmore[8], b. 1845, and Clarenc G. Dinsmore[8], b. 1848.

This closes a brief notice of some of the prom descendants of Robert Dinsmoor[4], son of John i moor[3], the captive of the Indians, who was the cl t son of John Dinsmoor[2], the Scotch lad who, with and broad bonnet, emigrated from the Tweed to B ly wattick, Ireland, who was son of *Laird* Dinsmoor[1] of Scotland.

David Dinsmoor[4] (name of father not known, but   grandson of John Dinsmoor[2], *Laird* Dinsmoor[1]), a nephew of John Dinsmoor[3], who settled in Londonderry, N. H., was b. in Ireland in 1714, emigrated to America about 1745, was in Londonderry, N. H., in 1747, m. Mrs. Kennedy, settled in Chester, N. H. His descendants live in Chester, Auburn, N. H., and Anson, Me. Among them is Rev. John Dinsmore. Some years ago Curran Dinsmore, Lemuel Dinsmore, and James P. Dinsmore, brothers, were living in New York and were his descen- dants.

DINSMOORS OF BALLYWATTICK, BALLY-MONEY, COUNTY ANTRIM, IRELAND.

12. Robert Dinsmoor[3] (5), John[2], *Laird* Dinsmoor[1]. He was b. in Ballywattick, Ballymoney, County Antrim, Ireland, presumably as early as 1673, and was a brother of John Dinsmoor[3], the first emigrant of the name to New Hampshire. He resided in Ballywattick, and was an intelligent, upright, and leading citizen. From a letter which I received Feb. 3, 1891, from Mr. William Hunter, of Ballywattick, I have obtained this information. Rev. R. Park was pastor of the Presbyterian Church there for over fifty years. On April 6, 1692, the church made application to the General Synod of Ulster for a minister, and made a second application in 1694. Then Rev. Hugh Kirkpatrick was appointed. He had fled to Scotland at the time of the Revolution, returned in 1695, and was installed over the church. In 1699 he was moderator of the Synod, and continued minister until his death, in 1712.

During his ministry, Robert Dinsmoor[3], the subject of this sketch, was a prominent member of his congregation, and was a member of a deputation* to the Synod at Antrim, County of Antrim, Ireland, in 1715, on matters relating to the church and congregation.

Details of his life are not known, nor the names of his wife and children. From his Christian name, from the fact of his residence in Ballywattick, his intelligence and education, his age, and the relation which his age bears to the subject of the following notice, it seems fair to infer that he was the father of the one whose sketch is here given (but there is no absolute proof), and so in that manner I have arranged them.

13. Robert Dinsmore[4], Robert[3] (?), John[2], *Laird* Dinsmoor[1]. He was a grandson of John Dinsmoor[2], the Scotch emigrant to Ballywattick, Ireland, and was b. in 1720; lived in Ballywattick, Ballymoney, County of Antrim, Ireland, the place of his birth, and was a farmer.

---

*The members of the delegation were as follows: Cornet Alexander McGown, Mr. James Henry, Allen Templeton, Robert Dinsmore, John Love, Peter Gamble, Thomas Reid, Quinton Dick, John Lawrence.

A brother lived near him, and each had a large fam
He was a leading man in the parish, was held in the hi
est respect, and was a Presbyterian in his religious bel
His intelligence was of a high order, and to him a c
indebted for the preservation of the genealogy and earl
history of the family. He was a man who enjoyed
ing, and during his life he kept up a correspondence
a Laird Dinsmoor, at the old home in Scotland, and
his relatives in New Hampshire, U. S. Among th
with whom he exchanged letters were John Dinsi o r
of Windham, N. H., and with his sons — John Dinsi o
whose wife was Susannah Bell, and Col. Silas Dinsmoor,
the celebrated Indian agent. Only one has bee i preserved, which was addressed to John Dinsmoor[6], of Wi l-
ham, N. H. (a part of the original Londonderry, N. H),
and printed with the book of poems of the "Rus c
Bard," Robert Dinsmoor, and dated : —

"BALLYWATTICK, Ireland, Aug. 12, 1   4

"My Dear Sir. — In July last, I received your affec
tionate letter of 22d Feb., 1794, where you have given
me a full and clear answer to my letter of May 12, 1793
which was directed to your honoured father, — but, alas!
no more. May I not bid adieu to North America.

"Submission is a duty, therefore I shall only add — I
shall go to him, but he shall not return to me. It gives
me consolation that he has left a son and heir, blessed
with his principles and talents. I see that you feel for
the commotions of Europe, and for the arbitrary proceed-
ings of our government in particular. You give them
hard names. Indeed, so could we, but dare not; we are
brought to submission indeed. While our lives are pro-
tected by the laws, we must submit our property to the
discretion of government without a murmur or complaint.
Provided our taxes, which are heavy, were disposed of
for internal defence of our country and encouragement of
our trade and manufactures, we would pay more cheer-
fully. But when we see it levied to support a ruinous
war, that we think Great Britain had nothing to do with,
we complain the more. At this moment the eyes of all
Ireland are looking earnestly for the completion of your

peace with Great Britain, on which the trade of Ireland
much depends. We know you have sent a late com-
missioner from Congress to the Court of Great Britain, a
Mr. Jay; but as nothing has yet transpired in respect to
Ireland, I must be silent. I had a long letter from your
brother Silas,* in May last, which I answered. It raises
my pride to find that there is a Dinsmoor in any part of
the globe so capable of composition as I see the writer of
this letter to be. The more so when I can truly call him
friend and cousin.

"As to your request concerning the genealogy of our
family, you have been pretty fortunate indeed in calling
on me, as I assure you there is not a man living within
my knowledge that can go as far up in that description
as I can. Nevertheless it may be short of what history
could afford. Please take the following: —

"My grandfather was born on the mean land of Scotland, near the River Tweed — the son of a wealthy farmer,
as I supposed from his style, being called the Laird of
Achenmead, as he had tenants under him. He had two
sons, of which my grandfather was the second, whose
name was John. He left his father's house in the seventeenth year of his age. I suppose he must have eloped,
as he brought no property with him, as I have often heard,
save a gray bonnet of great extent, with striped woollen
hose, and a small cane in his hand. This is your original
in Ireland, and mine; and all by the name of Dinsmore,
here or elsewhere, that belong to that stock. Therefore,
you will be ready to say, we have little to boast of. But
stay a little, my dear friend, and let us go a little higher,
and return to Scotland. You see, as above, we are
sprung from a farmer. Will this give us any dignity?
Yes; the most ancient, the most honorable in civil life.
The second man in creation was a farmer. Cain was a
tiller of the ground. What are Monarchs? What are
Kings, Dukes, Lords, Earls? What was Alexander, or
Philip of Macedonia, but murdering vagabonds?

"The character of a farmer is far above them all. Stop
but the farmer and his culture, and you sweep off the

---

* Col. Silas Dinsmoor, the Indian agent, and a brilliant man.

human race at one stroke. So you see that the 'a......'-
ssion is exalted above all others. Therefore, m.....
g..... is higher than any other whatever.

"I must crave your patience. Suffer me, then,.....
t..... to my grandfather and his offspring, of which y....a...
.... This man had four sons, John, Adam, Robert,
and Samuel. John was the first that migrated to Am....
i.... f the name, and the first that struck a stick ... I o
d......erry. This man was your grandfather's fa..... and
...y..e...t, who surmounted many difficulties in .....
a ....and free estate for his offspring, and in the .....
w..... ma le an Indian captive. Permit me to c...... .....
circumst.....ce with respect to my grandfather's .....ng
his father's house without any property, which m..... ....ei
d.. to the hint before observed, respecting it, which ....'s
I never heard this man give any other reason ....
for his leaving his father's house, but this: '.....u....a
father obliged him, and that uncovered, to hold..... e......
stirrup of his elder brother's saddle when he m.....n.... d
h......h.......rse. A subordination that appeared not t.... .....g...c
w..th this man's proud heart.

"May it not be an heir-ship entailed on his off-.......g.
And if so, whether virtue or vice, I leave with .....a to
determine, although I am no advocate for virtue .r vice
being hereditary. To conclude, then, this man l...l
until he was 99 (ninety-nine) years of age. He was fi'ty
years married, and twenty-nine years a widower .....h
ended his life, much respected by all who were acqu..... t.. l
with him, for his piety, morals, and good sense. Now
sir, I have gone as far as my memory could assist me in
answering your request. But there is yet som.'h..g
remains which may gratify your inquisitive mind, ... t....
line of heraldry. The Dinsmoor coat-of-arms is ....
laid down on a plate, of a green color, with three .....e....
sheaves set upright in the centre, of a yellow co......
emblematical of husbandry and agriculture.
                    "ROBERT DINSMOR...'

The grandfather of the person to whom the lette.... .s
addressed, Robert Dinsmoor[4], of Windham, N. H.... ...
an own cousin of Robert Dinsmore[4], the writer.

Another description is: "The picture of a man with
his dog and gun, with a sheaf of wheat and one of oats,
which crossed each other."* These are given for what
they are worth. They may amuse, but probably have no
historical value.

Mr. Dinsmore lived with his son, Samuel[5], the last of
his life, and died in Ballywattick, and is buried by the
side of his friends and kindred in the cemetery in Ballymoney, where there is a stone erected to his memory.
He was twice married. The first family went abroad,
and one son went with Capt. Cook around the world.
Nothing more is known of the first family of children or
their history.

CHILDREN, BORN IN BALLYWATTICK, IRELAND.

Second Family.

14. William Dinsmore[5], b. 1755, d. 1818, lived a long while in Philadelphia,
Penn. Returned to Ballymoney, Ireland; m. Jane Blair, and d.
there. No children. William Dinsmore owned a house and out-
buildings on Main Street, Ballymoney. In his barn Adam Clark,
the commentator, used frequently to hold religious services, at-
tended by many of the people. Mr. Dinsmore was a leading man
in the town, and was greatly respected. As he had no children,
the property which he possessed, which was considerable, went to
his relatives. The following is upon his tombstone in Ballymoney:
"Consigned to the tomb, in the 63d year of his age. Here lies the
remains of William Dinsmore, late of Ballywattick, a man distin-
guished by purity of morals and integrity of heart. Impressed
with a due sense of religion, his practice was regulated by its dic-
tates; firmly believing the truths of the Gospel his whole life
evinced the genuine fruit of Christianity, 1818."
15. Samuel Dinsmore[5] (19), b. 1761, lived in Ballywattick, Ballymoney,
Ireland, and d. Nov. 12, 1829. The father of John Dinsmore[6], of
Bloomington, Ind.
16. Molly Dinsmore[5], m. Thomas McIlhose, res. Derrock, County Antrim.
17. Margaret Dinsmore[5], m. Andrew Dinsmore (No. 41), of Ballywattick,
Ireland. He was her own-cousin.
18. Martha Dinsmore[4], m. Alexander Culberson, and lived in lower Ballywattick, Ireland.

19. Samuel Dinsmore[5] (15), Robert[4], Robert[3] (?),
John[2], Laird[1]. He was b. in Ballywattick, Ballymoney,
County Antrim, Ireland, in 1761; m. in 1783, Mary, daugh-
ter of Andrew Brewster, of Glenhall, County of London-
derry, Ireland. He was a large, tall, strong-limbed farmer,
and lived on a portion of the Dinsmore homestead in
Ballywattick, where he d. Nov. 13, 1829, and is buried in
Ballymoney Cemetery. Upon his tombstone in Bally-

* From letter of John Dinsmore[6] (grandson of foregoing Robert[4]), of
Bloomington, Indiana, dated Sept. 9, 1887.

money is this inscription : "Here lies the body of [...] Samuel Dinsmore, of Ballywattick, who depar[...] life the 13th Nov. 1829, aged 68 years; also, [...] Robert, who departed this life the 18th of Apr[...] aged 18 years." He and family were Presb[...] His widow died in Bloomington, Ind, in 18[...] lived in a comfortable stone house; at the end [...] a field surrounded by trees, which make the [...] tractive and home-like.

CHILDREN, BORN IN BALLYWATTICK, BALLYMONEY, COUNT[...] IRELAND.

20. William Dinsmore*, b. about 1785, lived in Ballywattick, [...] to America, and d. at Piqua, Miami Co., Ohio.

21. Andrew Dinsmore*, b. about 1877, res. at Charlottesville, he died suddenly; single.

22. Margaret Dinsmore*, b. about 1789; m. Archibald McI[...] lived in Ballywattick, on a farm occupied in 1891 by [...] then removed to Port Stewart, County of Londonderr[...] where they died. Two daughters are still living: Ma[...] reavy, single, res. Port Stewart, Ireland; Rachel McIlre[...] Mr. Reid, and has a large family, res. Cromnore. Coun[...] Ireland. Daniel McIlreavy went to Australia, and is d[...]

23. Bettie Dinsmore*, b. about 1791, m. Charles Riddle, and [...] burg, Penn. The family was there in 1890. See Histo[...]y dell, Riddle, Ridlon, Ridley, Family, p. 196, by G. T. Ri[...]

24. Samuel Dinsmore*, b. about 1792, was killed at Baltimore, [...] by being blown up in a powder mill.

25. James Dinsmore*, b. about 1795, d. in Hamilton, Ohio.

26. Robert Dinsmore*, b. about 1797, d. in Ballywattick, Irelan[...]

27. Mary Dinsmore*, b. about 1799, m. Samuel Johnson, a merc[...] lived and died at Bush Mills, Antrim. Ireland.

28. Jennie Dinsmore*, b. about 1803, m. Robert Small, and [...] in [...] burg, Penn. Her first husband was Mr. McAllist[...] daughter m. Mr. Pinkerton.* and they live in Philadelp[...]

29. Rachel Dinsmore*, b. about 1806, m. James McAffee; sh[...] Wooster, Ohio. His early home was near Giant's Caus[...]

30. Matilda Dinsmore*, b. about 1808, m. Campbell McCurdy [...] Baltimore, Md.

31. John Dinsmore* (32), b. in 1810, res. 1891, in Bloomington, In[...] following sketch of him and his family.

32. John Dinsmore[6] (31), Samuel[5], Robert[4], Rob[...] ert[3]?, John[2], *Laird* Dinsmoor[1]. He was b. in Bally-wattick, Ballymoney, County Antrim, Ireland, in 1810, and succeeded his father, on the home of his fo[...]athers, in the parish of his birth. There he remained several years after the death of his father and in 1838, he, the last of the name there, left his native land, the old home of his people for several generations, and with his famil[...]

and venerable mother removed to Bloomington, Ind., where he has ever since lived, and where he resides in April, 1891. Thus the ancestral home of the Dinsmores on Irish soil passed into the hands of others. It is occupied in 1891 by Archibald Usher. He and his family, his father and his family, are, and were, members of the Presbyterian Church. In a letter dated Oct. 1, 1890, he says : "I hope and trust, through the intercession of the Lord and Saviour Jesus Christ, that our names will be enrolled in the Book of Life." He m. in 1832, Margaret Small, who died in 1882, at Bloomington, Ind.

CHILDREN: THE THREE ELDEST BORN AT BALLYWATTICK, IRELAND; THE OTHERS AT BLOOMINGTON, IND.

23. Samuel Dinsmore[7], b. Feb. 8, 1834, m. Magdelene T. Hudsenpell, res. Burden, Kan. Children: John Dinsmore[8], Julia Dinsmore[8], Mary Dinsmore[8].
34. Joseph S. Dinsmore[7], b. Jan. 1, 1836, m. Mary A. Henderson, res. Bloomington, Ind. Children: Wadsey Dinsmore[8], William Dinsmore[8], Paul Dinsmore[8]. The two elder are in college at Bloomington, Ind.
35. Mary Dinsmore[7], b. January, 1838; d. Oct. 20, 1853, at Bloomington, Ind.
36. William J. Dinsmore[7], b. March 4, 1840, m. Mary Gates, res. Earlville, Ill. Children: Theophilus Dinsmore[8], Annie Dinsmore[8].
37. Andrew Dinsmore[7], b. February, 1842, d. May, 1843.
38. Jane Dinsmore[7], b. April 2. 1844, d. March, 1863.
39. Theophilus W. Dinsmore[7], b. Sept. 27, 1846, m. Sarah Bunger. He d. April 14, 1871.
40. Matilda H. Dinsmore[7], b. Jan. 4, 1850, m. Benjamin Kirby, res. Bloomington, Ind. They have one son and four daughters.

41. Andrew Dinsmore[5], ———[4], Robert[3](?), John[2], *Laird* Dinsmoor[1]. He lived in Ballywattick, in a stone house, now, 1891, unoccupied, and owned by Archibald Usher. He was a shrewd, sensible man, quite intelligent, and a man of influence in his neighborhood. He was a member, as were all the Dinsmores, of the Presbyterian Church of Ballymoney, which has been in existence since 1700. He died in the place of his nativity, and is buried with others of his kindred and name in the cemetery in the village of Ballymoney. He m. 1st, ——— ———, who had seven sons and one daughter. She died, and he m. 2d, his own-cousin, Margaret, daughter of Robert Dinsmore[4], *the letter writer.* On his tombstone in Ballymoney is: "Here rests the remains of Andrew Dinsmore, of Ballywattick, who departed this life 13th July,

1811, aged 73 years; and also his wife, Margaret wh.. died 4th April, 1813, aged 62 years. Much of the virtu - which ornament the Christian character were pos-esse by this Pair." They had seven daughters and one s The record of all his children, as given traditionally, is a follows, though some are missing.

CHILDREN, BORN IN BALLYWATTICK, BALLYMONEY, COUNTY ANTRIM, IRELAND.

42. John Dinsmore*, emigrated early to America, before 1817, and was government surveyor in one of the Southern States, where he resided He was m., but is said to have left no children;

43. Robert Dinsmore*, lived in Ballywattick. m. —— ——, died aft r the loss of his property with his brother-in-law, Joseph Small; l. about 1830, and is buried in Ballymoney. He had several children, among them Robert Dinsmore⁷, who settled in Tennessee; John Dinsmore⁷, William Dinsmore⁷, Elizabeth Dinsmore⁷, Margaret Dinsmore⁷, and Nancy Dinsmore⁷. They all came to Amer a after their father's death.

44. James Samuel Dinsmore*, b. 1771, d. in 1846. m. Jennie Herbert, and lived near Havre de Grace, Md., where his descendants a e said to be still living.

45. William Dinsmore*, called "Gentle Willie." He m. Martha Henry. He owned the farm and erected the stone house owned by William Knox in Ballywattick in 1891. He, "Gentle Willie," m with financial trouble, emigrated to Maryland, and died with his brother James. He had no children. His wife was from upper Secon, close to Ballywattick.

46. Andrew Dinsmore*, emigrated to America, before 1817. Tw other sons are said to have settled, one at Charlottesville, Va. a l ou farther South.

By Second Marriage with Margaret Dinsmore.

47. Rachel Dinsmore⁶ (52 , b. in 1810. m. John Hunter, res. York, Pen i.

48. Jane Dinsmore*, m. Joseph Small, lived in Ballywattick and in Knowend, County Antrim, Ireland. Farmer. Children : It s: said to have settled in Bloomington, Ind.

John Small⁷.
Joseph Small⁷.
Andrew Small⁷.
James Small⁷.
Rachel Small⁷, moved to Bloomington. Ind.
—— Small, m. —— Tomb. to Dunkendalt, Ballymoney antri n Ireland. Had a family, and removed to New England.
—— Small, m. Francis McKinley, of Strome, County Ant n ar Derrock, and removed to Bloomington, Ind.
—— Small, m. Mr. Smith, moved to Canada.
Margaret Small⁷, m. her cousin, John Dinsmore, removed t l an-Ington, Ind., in 1838. See sketch No. 32.

9. Mary Dinsmore*, m. Samuel Boyd, of Culbrom, County Antri . where they died. Child : Robert Boyd, went to United States Wes in United States Survey ; returned to County Down, and liv ! there. No family.

50. Susan (or Hannah) Dinsmore*, m, James Neill, of Dunken a, Bal-lymoney, County Antrim. He died, and his family re ed to Philadelphia, Penn. Children : James Neill⁷, Ann Neill Kache Neill⁷, Margaret Neill⁷.

51. —— Dinsmore, m. James Hay, of Burnside, Ballymoney unty Antrim. Children are deceased.

52. Rachel Dinsmore[6] (47), Margaret (Dinsmore[5]) Dinsmore[5], Robert[4], Robert[3] (?), John[2], *Laird* Dinsmoor[1]. She was b. in Ballywattick, Town of Ballymoney, County Antrim. Ireland, in 1810; m. John Hunter, son of John Hunter. of Secou. He was b. there 1784; was a weaver of fine linen. lived in Ballywattick. and built the house occupied in 1891 by William Hunter, his nephew. Went to America in 1817, and d. in York, Penn., in May, 1823, where they lived. Rachel (Dinsmore) Hunter m., second, Joseph McPherson, in 1829, and d. in York, Penn., Feb. 1, 1837. She and Mr. Hunter were members of the Presbyterian Church, and later she was a member of the Methodist Church.

CHILDREN.

53. **Rev. William Hunter[7]**, b. in Ballywattick, Ireland, May 26, 1811; m. Jane McCarty; went to America with his parents in 1817, became a clergyman in the Methodist Episcopal Church. and was an editor. He was a gifted man. and was a poet of merit. In alluding to another, in one of his sweet poems, he said:—

> Away from his home and the friends of his youth,
> He hasted. the herald of mercy and truth.
> For the love of his Lord. and to seek for the lost.
> Soon, alas! was his fall, but he died at his post.

> He asked not a stone to be sculptured with verse;
> He asked not that fame should his merits rehearse;
> But he asked as a boon. when he gave up the ghost,
> That his brethren might know that he died at his post.

He was author of the hymns,

> The Great Physician now is near,
> The sympathizing Jesus,

and of,

> Joyfully. joyfully, onward we move,
> Bound for the land of bright spirits above.

He d. in Cleveland, Ohio, Oct. 11, 1877. His second wife was Ursula McCarty, and he had children.

CHILDREN OF REV. WILLIAM HUNTER[7].

1. Rachel Dinsmore Hunter[8], d. in infancy.
2. Wesleyana Hunter[8], b. ——; m. Stephen Quinon, and d. in Pittsburg, Penn.. Oct. 8, 1839. Children: Mary Alice Quinon[9], b. Sept. 4, 1875; Flora Hunter Quinon[9], b. ——; d. Nov. 30, 1889.
3. Daniel McCarty Hunter[8]. b. June 2, 1840; m. ——, and res. Alliance. Ohio. No children.
4. Elliott Virginia Hunter[8]. b. ——; m. Dr. Volk; res. Riverside, Cal.
5. Leonidas Hamlin Hunter[8], b. June 18, 1844; m. Kate ——. Children: Flora Holmes Hunter[9], b. May 26, 1874; Bertha May Hunter[9], b. ——.
6. Flora Ursula Hunter[8], b. ——; m. Prof. Horace Bancroft. who d. She m., second, Stephen Quinon, recently, who is on the editorial staff of the Pittsburg Times. Children: Grove Hunter

Bancroft*. b. Oct. 29, 1867, d. Dec. 14, 1807; Leon I
Bancroft*. b. Oct. 17, 1868. Is night editor of Pitts
patch. Penn.; Edna Bella Bancroft* and Jennie Ella I
b. Sept. 4, 1870, Jennie d. Jan. 4, 1873; Ida Bancroft
4, 1872. d. Jan. 12, 1873; William Earl Bancroft*, b. M
res. Pittsburg, Penn.; Mabel Elizabeth Bancroft*,
1875, d. July 12, 1876.

7. John Andrew Hunter*. b. Dec. 1, 1847; m Hattie ——. C
    member of East Ohio Methodist Episcopal Confe
    signed, and is now a student of medicine at Colum
    Children: Andrew Dinsmore Hunter*, b. Jan. 27, 187
    Carey Hunter*. b. Aug. 21, 1874; Frank Dalles Hunte
    27, 1876. d. April 2, 1877; John Hunter*. b. Oct. 6, 1
    Lena Hunter*, b. Jan 1, 1880; Hattie Lillie Hunter
    1881, d. Aug. 23, 1882; Eva Mabel Hunter*, b. Se|
    Florence Lois Hunter*. b. Feb. 12, 1885; Gilbert Have
    b. April 4, 1887; Mary Vaughan Hunter*, b. Nov. 11,
8. Nathan Goff Hunter*. b. ——; d. in infancy.
9. Jane Amelia Hunter*, b. ——; m. Mr. Fordiug, a la
    near Riverside. Cal.

54. Rev. Andrew Hunter7, b. Ballywattick, Ireland, Dec. 26, 18
     America in 1817; m. Maria Jones. of York, Penn. He
     powerful clergyman in the Methodist Episcopal Chur
     degree of D. D. was conferred upon him. His ministry
     half a century. He was stricken with partial paralysis a
     Plant, Ark., while preaching, and is now partially reco
     home is near Bryant, fourteen miles from Little Rock, Ar

CHILDREN.

1. William Patterson Hunter*, res. near Bryant, Saline Co , Ark.; he
    was b. Sept. 21 1843.
2. Florence Bertrand Hunter*, b. Aug. 31, 1855; res. Little I c   Ark.
3. Andrew Jones Hunter*, b. April 8, 1858; res. Little Rock. Ari

55. John Hunter7, b. York, Penn., Oct. 15, 1817; m. Harriet McCarty He
     was a manufacturer. He was a strong. self-reliant man of busi-
     ness. was held in the highest esteem. and was an active member
     of the Methodist Episcopal Church; d. 1887; res. Alliance Ohio

CHILDREN.

1. Andrew Dinsmore Hunter*; deceased.
2. Elizabeth Hunter*; m. Erban Weikart, of Alliance, Ohi

56. Margaret Hunter7. was b. in York, Penn.. Oct. 31, 1820;   A g. 23,
     1842, Abram Wells, and res. in Wellsville. Penn. She s lives
     there in her pleasant home. "Willowdale," with h married
     daughters living near her. She is a lady of rare gifts and gr ces.
     Mr. Wells was a person of great courage and energy, b gh-souled,
     a.leader in society. and an example in all good works. d was
     atly missed and mourned at his death.

CHILDREN.

Emma Hunter Wells*, b. April 2, 1846; m. 1876, Fran s A uv
     Barrett of Wooster, Ohio, and has children: Willi   Hunter
     Barrett*, b. Oct. 28, 1877; Ruth Barrett*, b. Nov. 179. an l
     Margaret Barrett*, b. Sept. 27, 1881.
2. Olive Malinda Wells*, b. March 23, 1848; m. Dec. 23, 1 7 Robert
     John Belt, of Wellsville, Penn. Children, b. Wells Penn
     Abram Dinsmore Belt* and Margaret Dinsmore B t b. Oct
     27, 1871; James Edward Belt* and Miriam Alice Be b. May
     1881.
3. Harriet Maria Wells*, b. April 17, 1851; m. Aug 23, 1871. Fic a d
     Young, of New York, N. Y. Children: William Hunt :

Young[9], b. July 24, 1873. and d. Feb. 7. 1886. at Flatbush. L. I.; Olive Viola Young[9], b. Sept. 5, 1877, at Brooklyn. N. Y.; Richard Young[9], b. Sept 17. 1886.

4. Mary Dinsmore Wells[8], b. Nov. 10. 1854; m. June 1. 1876. Thomas Barkdale Hoover, of Wooster. Ohio; reside in the old home, "Willowdale," Wellsville. Penn. Their children are: Walter Wells Hoover[9], b. Oct. 13, 1877, at Wooster, Ohio; Thomas Leonard Hoover[9], b. Dec. 10, 1880, at Wellsville. Penn.; Donald Dinsmore Hoover[9] and Dorothy Geentner Hoover[9], b. Dec. 14, 1883; and Mary Elliotta Hoover[9], b. Aug. 21. 1885.

5. Margaret Wells[8], b. Dec. 23. 1856, at Wellsville. Penn.
6. Elliotta Wells[8], b. Feb. 14, 1861.
7. James G. Wells. of Wellsville. Penn., is a son of Abram Wells by a former marriage.
8. Adeline Emily Wells. daughter of Abram Wells by a former marriage. and was a most lovely woman. She m. Rev. D. C. John, a Methodist clergyman; and d. in Winona, Minn.. where she is buried. Children: Anna Miriam John. m. Mr. Armitage, res. Milwaukee, Wis.; James John; David John; William Nelson John.

57. Agnes Hunter[7]. the youngest child of Rachel Dinsmore[6] and her husband. John Hunter, was b. in York, Penn., May 15, 1822, and d. there in 18.2.

DINSMORES OF PENNSYLVANIA.

58. Adam Dinsmoor[3] * (6), John[2], *Laird* Dinsmoor[1]. He was b. in Ballywattick, Ballymoney, County Antrim, Ireland, presumably as early as 1675, and remained in Ireland, in the parish of his birth. He had three sons and perhaps other children. The sons emigrated to America and settled in Eastern Pennsylvania.

CHILDREN.

59. Robert Dinsmore[4]. At about the commencement of the Revolutionary War he removed to Western Pennsylvania, and settled on Miller's Creek, twelve miles southwest of Pittsburg. Later he removed to the unbroken wilderness of Kentucky, and his after history is unknown. In those early days there were no mails to those unknown borders of civilization, and little, if any. word was ever received by his friends after his departure from Pennsylvania.
60. James Dinsmore[4] (62). b. Ballywattick, Ireland, April 26, 1742; d. in Pennsylvania. in 1817.
61. Andrew Dinsmore[4] (86). b. Ballywattick, Ireland, in 1753; went to America and settled in York Co., Penn; d. April, 1829.

62. James Dinsmore[4] (60), Adam[3](?), John[2], *Laird* Dinsmoor[1]. He was b. April 26, 1742, in Ballywattick, Ballymoney, County Antrim, Ireland. He emigrated, in 1761, to York Co., Penn., and remained several years.

---

* He is supposed to be the father or grandfather of Robert[4], James[4], Andrew Dinsmore[4]. As my informant. Rev. John W. Dinsmore, D. D., of Bloomington. Ill.. thinks that Adam[3], or Robert[3], was their *father*, I have called Adam[3] their father, and have so numbered the generation.

About 1774. he and his brother, Robert, who w ,·n.
near him, removed to Miller's Creek, twelve mile ui-h-
west from Pittsburg, where he lived until 1794,   he
bought a large tract called Huntingdon Plantatior .
ton Top, Washington Co., Penn., some six miles n ν
from the town of Washington. It was, and i   ;
nificent tract of land, covered with enormous timber.
Where he first lived was, when he first settled there,
a howling wilderness, subject to frequent incursions of
the savages. The Dinsmoor family was one of the
first to invade the unbroken solitude, which now is one
of the richest and finest parts of the country. He was
of great size, weighing above three hundred pounds, and
a man of profound and exalted piety, an elder in the
Presbyterian Church, and of great influence in the entire
region where he lived   He d. on his estate in 1817, and
is buried in the churchyard at Upper Buffalo, six miles
west of Washington, Penn. He was twice m.; name of
first wife is unknown. He m., second, at Miller's Run,
Penn., Mary Walker. He changed the spelling of his
name to Dinsmore.

THEIR CHILDREN WERE: THOSE OF FIRST M. BORN YORK CO., PENN.;
BY SECOND M. AT MILLER'S CREEK. PENN.

63. Janaette Dinsmore⁵, b. Dec. 8, 1770; m. Mr. Lee; removed to Mendina, Ohio, and there died.
64. Elizabeth Dinsmore⁵, b. Dec. 24. 1772; m. ——.

By Second Marriage.

65. Mary Dinsmore⁵, b. May 29, 1777; m. Mr. Langhan, or Langdon.
66. John Dinsmore⁵ (70), b. July 14, 1779; m. Jane Carr.
67. James Dinsmore⁵ (76), b. March 4, 1782; m. Esther Hamilton.
68. Hannah Dinsmore⁵, b. Jan. 26, 1784; m. Mr. Saulsbury.
69. Sarah Dinsmore⁵, b. March 30, 1789; m. Thamas Mason. They had numerous and influential children, who were born at Cross Creek, Washington Co., Penn.

70. John Dinsmore⁵ (66), James⁴, Adam³ (?), Joh:
Laird Dinsmoor¹, previously mentioned, m. Jane Carr
in the autumn of 1800. Although not educated i tl
schools, he was a man of uncommon intelligence, of _· ··
dignity of character, of unusual force and energy, a ·· ·o'.
deep and fervent piety. For about fifty years he w   n
elder in the church, and had widely extended influei·c
He had a large and valuable estate, which had bee,ι his
father's. He completed a country house in 1810, of ·ι.οι·e

and brick, where died his parents, and himself and wife; but the mansion stands to-day, solid and impressive, and apparently will endure while the world does, unless it is destroyed by fire. Five generations of the family in its shelter have found a home. For eighty years it has been the abode of respectability and comfort, and of a large and free hospitality. He d. July 12, 1859.

HIS CHILDREN WERE BORN ON THE HOMESTEAD.

71. William Dinsmore[6] (80). b. Oct. 14, 1801; m. Rebecca, daughter of Capt. James Anderson, March 12, 1838.
72. James Dinsmore[6], b. May 20, 1803; m. Margaret Lyle, of Cross Creek, about 1827, and d. in 1873. He was a man of high character, wealth, and influence.
73. John Carr Dinsmore[6], b. Dec. 31, 1804; m. Lucinda Clutter, and d. about 1875.
74. Mary Carr Dinsmore[6], b. March 7, 1807; m. Samuel Cowan. They had numerous children, all deceased.
75. Robert W. Dinsmore[6], b. Aug. 1, 1810; m., first, Nancy Perrine; second, Matilda Clutter. The first wife of Robert W. Dinsmore[6] d. in a year, leaving a daughter, now Mrs. Nancy (Dinsmore[7]) Vance, of Washington, Penn. He had eight children by his second wife, all of whom d. in childhood, save one, Mrs. Ella (Dinsmore[7]) Phillips, of 2126 Michigan Avenue, Chicago, Ill. She and her widowed mother live together. Her father, Robert Dinsmore[6], was accounted a wealthy man, and on the night of Dec. 6, 1866, he was murdered by burglars in his own home and in the presence of his family, for which one of the murderers was hanged. His estate was near the old home.

76. James Dinsmore[5] (67), b. March 4, 1782; lived upon a portion of the elegant estate of his father, on Huntingdon Plantation, Canton Top, Washington Co., Penn. He had a numerous family. His wife was Esther Hamilton.

AMONG HIS CHILDREN ARE:

77. Mrs. Sarah (Dinsmore) Cook[6], of Washington Penn.
78. William W. Dinsmore[6], of West Middletown, Penn.
79. Alexander W. Dinsmore[6], of Bentonville, Ark., or Boonesboro, Ark. He is the father of Mr. Dinsmore[7], late U. S. Minister to Corea.

80. William Dinsmore[6] (71), John[5], James[4], Adam[3] (?), John[2], *Laird* Dinsmoor[1], was born on his father's famous estate, Huntingdon Plantation, Canton Top, Washington Co., Penn., Oct. 14, 1801, and died on the same spot, March 31, 1883. He was amiable and gentle, industrious and thrifty, of pure character, and greatly beloved. He was generous and hospitable, and a free giver to religious objects especially. He m. March 12, 1838, Rebecca, daughter of Capt. James Anderson, an officer of the Revolution. She d. Sept. 9, 1886, in her seventy-ninth year.

CHILDREN, BORN ON THE OLD HOMESTEAD.

81. Rev. John Walker Dinsmore[7], D. D., b. March 13, 1839. His advantages for education were the best, — academy, college, theological seminary, and by foreign travel. Rev. John W. Dinsmore, D. D., entered the Presbyterian University; ordained in 1863; was pastor at Prairie du Sac, Wis., from 1864 to 1870, and at Bloomington, Ill., since that time, having charge of a very large church of nearly seven hundred communicants. He m. Dec. 22, 1852, Adeline Vance, of the same Scotch-Irish blood as himself. Res. 315 East Street, Bloomington, Ill. Children: Three are deceased; those living are William Vance Dinsmore[8], b. March 30, 1868, graduated second in his class of one hundred and forty-one members at Princeton College, N. J., 1890, and he is in the engineers' department of the Burlington & Quincy R. R., Chicago, Ill.; Dudley Fitz-John Dinsmore[8], b. May 16, 1873, was educated at Lake Forrest Academy, Ill., in business, Bloomington, Ill.; Paul Anderson Dinsmore[8], b. Aug. 24, 1877, member of Illinois Normal University; Marguerita Adeline Dinsmore[8], b. Feb. 10, 1882.

82. Jane Melissa Dinsmore[7], b. May 1, 1841; m. Wilson McClean, of Washington, Penn., and has seven children.

83. Mary Virginia Dinsmore[7], b. May 1, 1841; m. J. H. McCarrell. Res. Lawrence, Kan. No living children.

84. James Anderson Dinsmore[7], b. July 2, 1844; d. in infancy.

85. William Malcolm Dinsmore[7], b. Jan. 25, 1843; m. his second cousin, Margaret, daughter of W. W. Dinsmore, and they reside on the old homestead at Huntingdon Plantation, Canton Top, Washington Co., Penn. They have four children.

86. Andrew Dinsmore[4] (61), Adam[3] (?), John[2], *Laird* Dinsmoor[1]. He was b. at Ballywattick, Ballymoney, County of Antrim, Ireland, in 1753, and emigrated to America when nineteen years of age, which would be in 1771–72, and settled at Peach Bottom, York Co., Penn., where he m. Catherine, only daughter of James Alexander. They lived there the remainder of

Records and history of different branches of the Dinsmoor family are printed in the following works, many of which can be found in the Library of the N. E. Historic and Genealogical Society, 18 Somerset Street, Boston, Mass., and in other antiquarian libraries:

Rev. Warren R. Cochrane's History of Antrim, N. H.
Hon. Leander W. Cogswell's History of Henniker, N. H.
Dinsmore Genealogy, published 1867, by Rev. John Dinsmore, of Winslow, Me.
Eaton's History of Thomaston, Me.
Genealogical and Historical Register, Vol. XVII.
Keyes' History of West Boylston, Mass.
Little Genealogy.
Hon. Leonard A. Morrison's History of Windham, N. H. A full history and genealogy of John Dinsmoor[3], the emigrant to Londonderry, N. H., and his descendants, 75 pp.; prepared by Hon. James Dinsmoor.
Page's History of Hardwick, Mass.
History of Washington, N. H.
Benjamin Chase's History of Chester, N. H.
For Dinsmores of Ireland, see Rambles in Europe, with Historical Facts Relating to Scotch-American Families, by Hon. Leonard A. Morrison, of Windham, N. H.
Rev. Thomas H. Dinsmore, D. D., Highland, Kan., is preparing a genealogy of his branch of the family.

their lives. He d. April. 1829, aged seventy-seven years
She was b. February, 1767; d. August, 1814, aged forty-
eight years

CHILDREN, BORN PEACH BOTTOM, YORK CO., PENN., POST OFFICE
SLATE RIDGE.

87. Jenny Dinsmore⁵ (97), b. Aug. 9, 1783; m. John Livingston. They lived
near Peach Bottom. and later removed to Ashland Co., Ohio.
88. Mary Dinsmore⁵. b. Feb. 9, 1786; she m. Mr. Scott. Children : Rev.
John W. Scott⁶. D. D., LL. D.; was President of Washington College, Penn., and d. some years ago; Rev. James Scott⁶. They
were successful teachers, as well as prominent clergymen of the
Presbyterian Church.
89. James Alexander Dinsmore⁵ (111), b. March 20, 1788; m. Grizzel Collins; res. Ashland Co.. Ohio.
90. Rachel Dinsmore⁵, b. Jan. 9, 1791; m. Mr. Kerr, of York Co., Penn.
Child: Kitty Ann Kerr⁶.
91. William Dinsmore⁵, b. Feb. 15, 1794; single; d. when a young man.
92. Martha Dinsmore⁵ (119.), b. Jan. 22, 1797; m. David Mitchell, of York
Co., Penn.
93. Andrew Dinsmore⁵ (124), b. June 10, 1799; physician and teacher; d.
March 3, 1808.
94. Anne Alexander Dinsmore⁵ (125). b. June 26. 1801; m. Rev. Benjamin
Mitchell, D. D., of York Co., Penn.; d. Mt. Pleasant, Ohio, June,
1842.
95. Samuel Dinsmore⁵ (132), b. April 4. 1804; m. Cecilia M. Williamson,
of Peach Bottom, York Co . Penn.; res. Slaterville. York Co . Penn.
96. Robert Caldwell Dinsmore⁵ (141), b. July 28, 1807; m Rebecca Kilgore;
res. Peach Bottom, York Co., Penn.

97. Jenny Dinsmore⁵ (87), Andrew⁴, Adam³ (?),
John², *Laird* Dinsmoor¹. She was b. at Peach Bottom.
York Co., Penn., Aug. 9, 1783; m. John Livingston,
who resided near that place. They removed to Ashland
County, Ohio, in 1836, where they died.

CHILDREN.

98. Andrew Livingston⁶, was a physician.
99. Sarah Jane Livingston⁶.
100. Mary Livingston⁶, m. Rev. Jacob Wolf, of Hawpatch, LaGrange
Co.. Ind.
101. John Livingston⁶.
102. Hugh Livingston⁶.
103. Catherine Livingston⁶.
104. William Livingston⁶, d. when young.
105. Anne Livingston⁶.
106. James Livingston⁶, d. when young.
107. Nancy Livingston⁶.
108. Martha Livingston⁶, m. Rev. J. Ross Ramsey, of York County, Penn.
109. William S. Livingston⁶. was a clergyman.
110. James Robert Livingston⁶.

111. James Alexander Dinsmore⁵ (89), Andrew⁴,
Adam³ (?), John². *Laird* Dinsmoor¹. He was b. at
Peach Bottom, York Co., Penn., March 20, 1788. En-
listed as a soldier in the war of 1812–15, and with his

company marched to the defence of Fort McHenry, at
Baltimore. In 1814 he went to Ohio, and entered a half-
section of land in Ashland Co., when he returned to
Pennsylvania, where he lived till 1833, on a farm on
Muddy Creek, near his father's, at Peach Bottom, York
Co., when he and his family removed to his farm of three
hundred and twenty acres, on the Muddy Fork, in Jackson, Ashland Co., Ohio., making the long journey through
the then wilderness and over the mountains in a wagon,
his wife, with a babe in her arms, riding most of the way
on horseback. He and his wife were members of the
Presbyterian Church, and adorned their profession by
godly lives, living in peace with all men. He d. in Jackson, Ohio, Jan. 7, 1863, and his wife Jan. 20, 1888. Mrs.
Dinsmore's maiden name was Grizzell, a daughter of David
and Dorcas (Neal) Collins, of Chanceford, York Co.,
Penn., a runaway couple. Her father was b. 1768; d.
March 26, 1828. Her mother was b. Jan. 5, 1778; d.
March 6, 1874. She was b. Aug. 23, 1799, and m. Mr.
Dinsmore March 14, 1826.

CHILDREN: THE FOUR ELDEST WERE BORN IN PEACH BOTTOM, YORK
CO., PENN.; THE REST IN JAKCSON, ASHLAND CO., OHIO.

112. Catherine Ann Dinsmore[6] (145), b. Feb. 8, 1827; m. May 2, 1848, Augustus Moore Hay, who d. Nov. 26, 1850, leaving one child. She
m. second, William Collins, who lived on a farm near Xenia, Green
Co., Ohio, where their four children were born.
113. Tabitha Mary Dinsmore[6] (150), b. Oct. 14, 1828; m. April 23, 1856, Hon.
Thomas Beer. Res. Bucyrus, Crawford Co., Ohio.
114. David Collins Dinsmore[6] (160), b. Dec. 10, 1830; m. April 2, 1863,
Cyrilla Andrews.
115. Janette Elizabeth Dinsmore[6], b. April 16, 1833; m. Nov. 1, 1865,
Joseph R. Reed, of Adel, Dallas Co., Iowa. She d. July 27, 1887,
at Council Bluffs, Iowa. She was a member of the Presbyterian
Church, of which her husband was an elder, and was faithful unto
death. Mr. Reed was elected Judge of the Court of Common
Pleas for two terms, then Judge of the Supreme Court, and was
chosen to Congress in 1888.
116. Andrew Alexander Dinsmore[6] (171), b. Aug. 7, 1835; m. Oct. 13, 1864,
Margaret A. Woodburn; clergyman. Res. Alhambra, Cal.
117. Rachel Margaret Dinsmore[6], b. March 20, 1838. Res. West Salem,
Wayne Co., Ohio. She was educated at Vermillion Institute,
Hayesville, Ashland Co., Ohio; was then a teacher, then relin-
quished her work, and for twenty years cared for her invalid
mother.
118. James Robert Washington Dinsmore[6] (176), b. Dec. 16, 1840; m. in
1890, Mrs. Mary Heacock.

119. Martha Dinsmore[5] (92), Andrew[4], Adam[3] (?),
John[2], *Laird* Dinsmoor[1]. She was b. at Peach Bottom,
York Co., Penn., Jan. 22, 1797; m. May 17, 1821,

David Mitchell, b. at Peach Bottom, Penn., Aug. 24, 1796. He was an elder in the church, and d. April 20, 1881. She d. March 24, 1862.

CHILDREN, ALL BORN AT PEACH BOTTOM, PENN.

120. Rev. Andrew Dinsmore Mitchell[6]. b. Feb. 22, 1824; was a Chaplain in the regular army; d. at Fort Grant. Ari., of apoplexy. March 26, 1882. He m. Oct. 15, 1854. Mary Neistling. of Middletown. Dauphine Co., Penn., and left a son. Prof. B. W. Mitchell[7], A. M., Ph. D., of Allegheny (Penn.) Academy. He was b. March 24, 1861. He m. Annie Lee Edwaids. of Cumberland, Penn.; res. at No. 18 Arch Street, Allegheny. Penn.
121. Joseph Rodney Mitchell[6]. b. Nov. 21, 1825; m. Sept. 5, 1870. Celia C. Grove. of St. Clairsville. Ohio. They have five children: Carrie Dinsmore Mitchell[7], b. Sept. 4, 1873; Mary M. Mitchell[7], b. March 4, 1876; Rodney Mitchell[7], b. June 4, 1878; Blanche G. Mitchell[7], b. Nov. 30, 1881; Helen Cecelia Mitchell[7], b. Nov. 16, 1884. Joseph Rodney Mitchell resides at St. Clairsville, Ohio, where all his children were born.
121a. Mary Catherine Mitchell[6], b. Feb. 16, 1831; d. March 8, 1834.
122. Martha Ann Mitchell[6], b. Oct. 1, 1833; res. Woodbine, York Co., Penn.
123. Elizabeth Susan Harper Mitchell[6], b. April 12, 1838; m. March 11, 1880. James P. Mitchell; res. Woodbine, York Co., Penn.

124. Andrew Dinsmore[5] (93), Andrew[4], Adam[3] (?), John[2], *Laird* Dinsmoor[1]. Born at Peach Bottom. York Co., Penn., June 10, 1799; never married. Graduated at the College at Schenectady, N. Y., became a physician, and for many years practised his profession in a hospital at Baltimore, Md. Afterward he established a school for boys at Shrewsbury, York Co., Penn., where he was a successful teacher. He d. March 3, 1868.

125. Anne Alexander Dinsmore[5] (94), Andrew[4], Adam[3] (?). John[2], *Laird* Dinsmoor[1]. She was b. at Peach Bottom, York Co., Penn., June 26, 1801; m. April 26, 1826. Rev. Benjamin Mitchell, D. D., b. Nov. 25, 1800, of York Co., Penn. They removed to Mt. Pleasant, Jefferson Co.. Ohio, where he preached more than fifty years to one congregation, and died greatly beloved at an advanced age. at Mt. Pleasant, Ohio, Dec. 26, 1884. She d. June, 1842.

CHILDREN.

126. Catherine Mitchell[6], m. Rev. Joseph Thoburn, of Wheeling, W. Va. He was Colonel of a regiment. promoted to Brigadier-General. and was killed while in the United States service.
127. Mary R. Mitchell[6].
128. Addison Mitchell[6].
129. Andrew Mitchell[6].
130. Eliza Mitchell[6].
131. Martin Mitchell[6].

132. Samuel Dinsmore[5] (95), Andrew[4], Adam[3] (?),
John[2], *Laird* Dinsmoor[1]. He was b. at Peach Bottom,
York Co., Penn., April 4. 1804 ; m. June 13, 1837, Cecilia
M., daughter of Peter and Elizabeth (Steele) Williamson,
b. Sept. 21, 1816, at Peach Bottom. Penn., and resided at
Peach Bottom, York Co., Penn.. where he died April 29,
1875. She res. at Peach Bottom, Penn.

CHILDREN.

133. Catherine Elizabeth Dinsmore[6], b. April 17, 1838; m. Dec. 12, 186)., Robert N. Glasgow; res. Peach Bottom, Penn. She d. March 13, 1870.
134. Rachel Anna Dinsmore[6], b. March 11, 1840; single; res. Peach Bottom, Penn.
135. James Scott Dinsmore[6], b. Feb. 25, 1842; res. Peach Bottom, Penn. ; m. June. 1872, Sarah Kilgore, who died. He m. second, Sarah Ferguson.
136. John Calvin Dinsmore[6], b. Sept. 23, 1844; res. Delta, Penn.; single ; farmer.
137. Peter Andrew Dinsmore[6], b. March 10, 1850; was a physician; single. He died at Deadwood. Dak., Sept. 23, 1877.
138. Margaret Marcelina Dinsmore[6], b. Aug. 18, 1852; m. June 6, 1883, James Scarborough; res. near Pittsburg, Penn.; farmer.
139. William Samuel Dinsmore[6], b. March 6, 1855; res. once at Delta, Penn. He m. Mary Cooper, August, 1882. Res. Smithsburg, Md. ; teacher.
140. Thomas Robert Dinsmore[6], b. June 29, 1857; d. Feb. 5, 1858.

141. Robert Caldwell Dinsmore[5] (96), Andrew[4],
Adam[3] (?), John[2], *Laird* Dinsmoor[1]. He was b. at
Peach Bottom, York Co., Penn., July 28, 1807 ; m.
Rebecca Kilgore. of Chanceford, York Co., Penn.; res.
at Peach Bottom, Penn., until their death. He d. Dec.
8, 1863. She d. Dec. 16, 1854. Three children died in
infancy.

CHILDREN.

142. John Andrew Dinsmore[6], b. April 17, 1834; m. Feb. 1, 1860, Sarah Elizabeth Ramsay, b. May 10, 1836. He d. in Aberdeen, S. Dak., Sept. 27, 1888.

CHILDREN.

1. Rebecca Margaret Dinsmore[7], b. Nov. 19, 1860.
2. Jennie Augusta Dinsmore[7], b. March 12, 1863; m. Jan. 15, 1890, in Aberdeen, S. Dak., Edward E. McConkey, of Peach Bottom, Penn.
3. Carrie Nelson Dinsmore[7], b. May 22, 1865.
4. Annie Mary Dinsmore[7], b. Sept. 7, 1867.
5. Ross Alexander Dinsmore[7], b. June 23, 1870.

143. Samuel Nelson Dinsmore[6], b. at Peach Bottom, July 23, 1836; d. July 9, 1863, at Portsmouth, Va.; school teacher; single.
144. Robert Alexander Dinsmore[6], b. Sept. 14, 1840, at Peach Bottom; res. Delta, York Co., Penn. He m. March 7, 1872, at Peach Bottom, Penn., Annie Maria Watson, b. there Nov. 12, 1850. She was the daughter of Thomas Alexander and Helen (Beattie) Watson, of Peach Bottom. Her father was born in Wilmington, Del., son of

James and Margaret (McAllister) Watson, of Wilmington. James was son of Thomas Watson, of the North of Ireland. Mr. Dinsmore is a farmer and resides at Peach Bottom, Penn., on the homestead of his father, once owned by Andrew Dinsmore[4], the Emigrant.

CHILDREN, BORN AT PEACH BOTTOM, YORK CO., PENN., EXCEPT THE TWO YOUNGEST.

1. Helen Margaret Dinsmore[7], b. Dec. 12. 1872.
2. Nelson Caldwell Dinsmore[7]. b. Sept. 11, 1874.
3. James Watson Dinsmore[7], b. July 19, 1876.
4. Walter Scott Dinsmore[7], b. Sept. 25. 1878.
5. Rebecca Kilgore Dinsmore[7], b. April 28, 1880.
6. Chester McAllister Dinsmore[7], b. May 3. 1882.
7. Thomas Howard Dinsmore[7], b. Jan. 15, 1884.
8. Marian Belle Dinsmore[7], b. Jan. 19, 1887.

145. Catherine Ann Dinsmore[6] (112), James Alexander[5], Andrew[4], Adam[3] (?), John[2], *Laird* Dinsmoor[1]. She was b. in Peach Bottom, York Co., Penn., Feb. 8, 1827; m. May 2, 1848, Augustus Moore Hay, who d. Nov. 26, 1850. She m. second, April 25, 1861, William Collins, of ———, Green Co., Ohio, who d. July 18, 1887. Mrs. Collins d. Dec. 28, 1887. They were members of the United Presbyterian Church.

CHILDREN.

146. Henrietta Grizzell Hay[7], b. Aug. 14, 1850; m. ———; res. Springfield Ohio.
146a. Dinsmore Smart Collins[7], b. April 13, 1862.
147. Mitchell Wilberforce Collins[7], b. Sept. 20, 1863.
148. Clarkson Beer Collins[7], b. July 28, 1867.
149. William Augustine Collins[7], b. April 16, 1870; d. in infancy.

150. Tabitha Mary Dinsmore[6] (113), James Alexander[5], Andrew[4], Adam[3] (?), John[2], *Laird* Dinsmoor[1]. She was b. at Peach Bottom, York Co., Penn., Oct. 14, 1828; m. April 23, 1856, Thomas Beer, son of Rev. Thomas Beer, D. D., a Presbyterian clergyman; res. Bucyrus, Crawford Co., Ohio. He was a member of the Ohio Legislature from Crawford County in 1863, of the Constitutional Convention in 1873, Judge of the Court of Common Pleas in 1874 and subsequent years, and Judge of the Circuit Court in 1884 and 1886 for full term of six years.

CHILDREN.

151. Mary Margaret Beer[7], b. March 26, 1857; d. Jan. 12, 1866.
152. James Dinsmore Beer[7], b. Sept. 15, 1858; m. Sept. 2, 1884, Jean Lyle Thoburn, of Mount Pleasant, Ohio; physician; res. Wooster, Ohio.

1. Mary Margaret Beer[8].
2. Thomas Beer[8].

153. Thomas Cameron Beer[7], b. Sept. 14, 1860.
154. William Collins Beer[7], b. Jan. 23, 1863; m. May 19, 1886, Martha Alice Baldwin, at Council Bluffs, Iowa; is in the Omaha National Bank; res. Omaha, Neb.

1. Alice B. Beer[8].
2. Thomas Beer[8].

155. Dorcas Grizzell Beer[7], b. Dec. 31, 1865.
156. Katherine Janette Beer[7], b. May 13, 1868.
157. Robert L. Beer[7], b. Aug. 9, 1870.
158. Infant daughter[7], b. August 9, 1870; d.
159. Mary Elizabeth Beer[7], b. Aug. 10, 1875.

160. David Collins Dinsmore[6] (114), James Alexander[5], Andrew[4], Adam[3] (?), John[2], *Laird* Dinsmoor[1]. He was b. at Peach Bottom, York Co., Penn., Dec. 10, 1830; m. April 2, 1863, Cyrilla Andrews. He studied medicine in Cleveland, Ohio; was three years in the army, and was Captain in an Iowa regiment; is now practising his profession, and resides in Kirkville, Iowa.

161. Infant son[7], b. and d. Dec. 21, 1864.
162. James Andrew Dinsmore[7], b. May 30, 1866; d. April 2, 1868.
163. Jessie Dinsmore[7], b. May 12, 1867.
164. Katherine Louisa Dinsmore[7], b. July 18, 1868; d. Aug. 20, 1868.
165. Clara Dinsmore[7], b. July 4, 1869.
166. Henry Dinsmore[7], b. Dec. 17, 1870.
167. Mary Dinsmore[7], b. Aug. 28, 1872; d. March 2, 1873.
168. Florence Dinsmore[7], b. Oct. 28, 1873.
169. Henrietta Dinsmore[7], b. Nov. 10, 1874.
170. Helen Dinsmore[7], b. Sept. 20, 1876.

171. Rev. Andrew Alexander Dinsmore[6] (116), James Alexander[5], Andrew[4], Adam[3] (?), John[2], *Laird* Dinsmoor[1]. He was b. at Rowsburg, Ashland Co., Ohio, Aug. 7, 1835; m. Oct. 13, 1864. Margaret Ann Woodburn, b. Aug. 11, 1842, daughter of John and Jane (Hutchinson) Woodburn, of Freeport, Armstrong Co., Penn. He graduated at Jefferson College, Canonsburg, Penn., in 1860, and in 1863 from the Western Theological Seminary, at Allegheny, Penn., and was, in 1862, licensed to preach by the Wooster Presbytery of Ohio. During the war, was twice at the front in the service of the Christian Commission; in November and December, 1863, at the battle of Chattanooga, Tenn., and in April and May, 1865, at City Point, Va. In 1864 was ordained and installed over the Presbyterian Church at Neenah, Wis. In November, 1866, was called to First Presbyterian Church at Des Moines, Iowa, where he spent five years. Was pastor of church in Milford, Del., in 1873, and in 1876 was called to Bridesburg, Philadelphia, Penn., where he remained about twelve years. Went to California in 1887, and on July 17, 1889, he took the pastorate of the First Presbyterian Church in his present home. Res. Alhambra, Los Angeles Co., Cal.

CHILDREN.

172. William Alexander Dinsmore[7], b. Des Moines, Iowa, Jan. 5, 1867; single; res. Sioux City, Iowa; banker.
173. Frank Woodburn Dinsmore[7], b. Des Moines, Iowa, Nov. 4, 1869; res. Sioux City, Iowa; merchant.
174. Howard Collins Dinsmore[7], b. Milford, Del., July 3, 1875; d. Philadelphia. Penn., Dec. 9, 1876.
175. Mabel Lulu Dinsmore[7], b. Philadelphia, Penn., May 10, 1881; res. Alhambra, Cal.

176. James Robert Washington Dinsmore[6] (118), James Alexander[5], Andrew[4], Adam[3] (?), John[2], *Laird* Dinsmoor[1]. He was b. Jackson, Ashland Co., Ohio, Dec. 16, 1840. He served three years in the Union Army, and was three times wounded. He m. 1890, Mrs. Mary Heacock. He was educated at the Vermillion Institute, Hayesville, Ashland Co., Ohio; res. on the homestead at Jackson, Ashland Co., Ohio; owns a portion of the farm of his father, and has one child.

DINSMORES OF PENNSYLVANIA.

177. Robert Dinsmore[4], —— Dinsmore[3], John[2], *Laird* Dinsmoor[1]. He was b. in the North of Ireland, probably in Ballywattick, Ballymoney, County Antrim. He was of pure Scotch blood, and, according to tradition, was the son or grandson of Robert Dinsmoor[3] (5), Adam Dinsmoor[3] (6), or Samuel Dinsmoor[3] (7), the three brothers of John Dinsmoor[3] (4) who emigrated to New Hampshire as early as 1723. These four brothers, as has been stated, were sons of John Dinsmoor[2], who emigrated from Scotland to Ireland, who was son of *Laird* Dinsmoor[1], who lived upon the River Tweed.

According to the information which we have, the afore-said Robert Dinsmoor[3], Adam Dinsmoor[3], and Samuel Dinsmoor[3] were, with their children, and Robert Dinsmoor[4], who emigrated to New Hampshire in 1731, the only Dinsmoors in that section of country at that period, from 1722 to 1726; so I have called Robert Dinsmore[4], the subject of this sketch, of the fourth generation. By tradition he was a cousin of Robert[4], James[4], and Andrew Dinsmoor[4], who had preceded him a score or more of years and settled in Pennsylvania. (See p. 19.)

Mr. Dinsmore[4] m. Nancy, daughter of Moses Scott, also of Scotch blood. Her father lived in, or near, the City of Londonderry, Ireland. He and his wife were members of the Presbyterian Church, and both were dis-tinguished for intelligence, piety, and strict adherence to the church of their forefathers. After marriage they lived in the County of Donegal, on the Lough or River Foyle, three miles below the City of Londonderry, Ire-land,* where nine children were born to them. They were lovers of liberty and haters of the annoyances, civil, religious, and political, incident to their abode in Ireland. So, in 1790, Mr. Dinsmore and his sons, John[5] and Robert[5], sought and found a home in the new Republic. During their absence, Mrs. Dinsmore died, when his eldest daughter, Mary[5], with the others, settled up the business, and, following the direction of their father, these seven children set sail for the United States, arrived in 1792, and settled in Peach Bottom, York Co., Penn., about 1800 or 1801. He removed to Allegheny Co., and set-tled on a farm on Turtle Creek, about twelve miles east of Pittsburg, where, as a farmer, he spent the remainder of his life. He had been a farmer in Ireland.

In his eighty-third year he m. second, Mrs. Margaret (Acheson) Stewart, Nov. 16, 1805, and they had three children. She was a native of the North of Ireland.

___

* On the afternoon of Wednesday, March 27, 1884, I met, in the City of Londonderry, Ireland, James Dinsmoor and his two sons from Muff, in the County of Donegal, Ireland, on Lough or River Foyle, and three miles from the City of Londonderry. The Christian names of James, John, and Ephraim frequently appeared in that branch of the Dinsmoor family. Their home was certainly not far from the place from which emigrated Robert Dinsmoor[4], to Pennsylvania.—[LEONARD A. MORRISON.

He was a man of great activity, energy, and force; was hale and stout in his old age, and carried forward successfully the business of his farm. He was severely injured by the fall of his horse, and died in 1817, between ninety and ninety-five years of age. His wife survived him, and died April 4, 1842. His tomb is in the cemetery of the Beulah Presbyterian Church, of which he and his wife were members. The first family of children grew to adult age, married, and had families, except the eldest daughter, who died in young womanhood.

CHILDREN.

178. John Dinsmore⁵, m. Martha Pollock, soon after his arrival in Pennsylvania, 1790. He settled in the country in York Co., where he d. early in the present century. He had two sons and one daughter.
179. Robert Dinsmore⁵, m. Feb. 28, 1827, Margaret Curry, and settled on a farm on Pucketaw Creek, Westmoreland Co., Penn., where he d. aged about eighty years.

CHILDREN.

1. Robert Dinsmore⁶, m. Mary Livingston, and left nine children, eight of whom arrived at maturity, and four became teachers.

CHILDREN.

I. Margaret C. Dinsmore⁷, m. A. M. Wolff. Children: Rev. Dr. A. F. Wolff⁸, pastor of the First Presbyterian Church; res. Alton, Ill. Robert Dinsmore Wolff⁸, res. Greensburg, Westmoreland Co., Penn.; is local editor of the "Greensburg Press." Elizabeth Dinsmore Wolff⁸, is not married.
II. Robert Scott Dinsmore⁷, b. July 11, 1829, in Plum Top, Allegheny Co., Penn.; has been a teacher most of his life; now a farmer and Justice of the Peace. He m. April 18, 1861, Isabella Christy, daughter of David Christy of Plum Top, Penn., who d. May 9, 1863; two sons, one deceased. He m. second, Sept. 3, 1867, Sarah Jane McKee. Mr. Dinsmore, his wife, daughter, and three eldest sons, are members of the Presbyterian Church. Children: John Hamilton Dinsmore⁸, b. Jan. 31, 1862; m. Sept. 19, 1888, Nettie Wilson, of Minnesota; farmer; res. Maine. Otter Tail Co., Minn. Harry Homer Dinsmore⁸, b. Sept. 6, 1868; student in Greensburg Seminary, Penn. William McKee Dinsmore⁸, b. March 15, 1870; at home; farmer. Mary Alice Dinsmore⁸, b. April 11, 1872. Robert Ross Dinsmore⁸, b. Sept. 24, 1874. Clarence Carey Dinsmore⁸, b. May 17, 1877. Alexander Cooke Dinsmore⁸, b. Nov. 28, 1879. Benjamin Scott Dinsmore⁸, b. Sept. 6, 1882.
III. Mattie Robinson Dinsmore⁷, m. Alexander Cooke, and d. March 7, 1888.
IV. Mary Livingston Dinsmore⁷, m. Hugh Donnell. Children: Robert Dinsmore Donnell⁸, res. Richmond, Ind. Rebecca Donnell⁷, res. with her parents in Verona, Allegheny Co., Penn.
V. James Livingston Dinsmore⁷, b. Feb. 1, 1835; d. April 30, 1888; single.
VI. Sarah Ross Dinsmore⁷, res. Shenandoah, Iowa.
VII. Nannie M. Dinsmore⁷, m. August, 1881, Benjamin Walp. He died. She res. Shanandoah, Iowa.
VIII. Rebecca Alter Dinsmore⁷, m. Robert H. Adams; res. Canton, Ohio.

2. **Margaret Curry Dinsmore⁵**, m. Hon. Joseph Alter, of Parnassus, Westmoreland Co., Penn., and had

CHILDREN.

I. David Alter⁷, b. Dec. 28, 1829; m. Mary Anderson, Dec. 31, 1863. He is a successful physician and has been in practice since 1865. He graduated at Jefferson Medical College, in Philadelphia, Penn., March 9, 1861, and was surgeon of the 206th Regiment of Pennsylvania Volunteers during the war. He res. Parnassus, Penn Children: Alonzo Anderson Alter⁸, b. March 10, 1865; is a member of the class of '92, at Princeton College, N J. William Irvine Alter⁸, is in business at 704 Eighth Avenue, New York City. He was manager and proprietor of the "Parnassus Press" for two years. Joseph Alter⁸, is a member of the class of '94, at Westminster College, New Wilmington, Lawrence Co., Penn.

II. Robert Dinsmore Alter⁷, b. July 18, 1839; m. Elizabeth, daughter of John McKean, of Burrell, Penn., and d. February, 1887. Children: Maggie Viola Alter⁸; Randall Murray Alter⁸; James Clarence Alter⁸. They all live at Parnassus, Penn.

III. Rev. Joseph Alter⁷, b. Dec. 18, 1841; was a member of the 123d Regiment of Pennsylvania Volunteers; was wounded at the battle of Fredericksburg; graduated at the University of Wooster, Ohio. June 25, 1873, and at the U. P. Theological Seminary, at Allegheny. Penn.; was licensed to preach April 18, 1876; ordained at Valley Falls, Dec. 12, 1877, and was pastor there and at Waterville for seven years; was a missionary in Washington Territory until 1891, when he was appointed to the Indian Mission at Warm Springs, Crook Co., Ore., where he res. April, 1891. He m. Jeanette Copley, Nov. 25, 1886. Children: Wade Dinsmore Alter⁸, b. March 25, 1888; Margaret Truby Alter⁸, b. Nov. 11, 1889.

IV. Maria Alter⁷, m. Martin Van Buren, a grandson of the late President Van Buren. He is a farmer, an elder in the Presbyterian Church, and res. at Forest, Hardin Co., Ohio. Children: Robert Van Buren⁸; Carl Van Buren⁸; Kent Van Buren⁸; Ethel Van Buren⁸; Hattie Van Buren⁸.

V. Nancy Alter⁷, who lived to adult age.
VI. Margaret Alter⁷, who lived to adult age.
VII. Elizabeth Alter⁷, who lived to adult age.
VIII. Rebecca D. Alter⁷, who lived to adult age.
IX. Mary Jane Alter⁷, d. in infancy.
X. Jane Alter⁷, d. in infancy.
XI. Lucinda Ann Alter⁷, d. in infancy.

180. Mary Dinsmore⁵, d. unmarried in early woomanhood.
181. Jane Dinsmore⁵, m. James Garvine; res. Ohio Co., ten miles south of Wheeling, W. Va.

CHILDREN.

1. John Garvine⁶, m. 1834. Helen Ritchie; lived in Guernsey Co., near New Cumberland. Ohio; d. 1882, leaving eight children.
2. Moses Dinsmore Garvine⁶, m. Miss Phillips. Child: William Garvine, who is married and has children. Res. Cambridge, Guernsey Co., Ohio.
3. James Garvine⁶, d. in Weston, Mo., leaving two sons.
4. Mary Garvine⁶, m. Martin Kellar; res. Bridgeport, Ohio. She left several children.
5. Rachel Garvine⁶, m. —— Smith, M. D.

182. Henry Dinsmore⁵, m. 1806, Sarah Ross; lived on a farm near Turtle Creek, Allegheny Co., Penn., where he died about 1846; ten children; four died in infancy and the others arrived at maturity.

CHILDREN.

1. Nancy Scott Dinsmore[6], m. March 1, 1827, Hamilton Stewart. They left eleven children.
2. Margaret Dinsmore[6], m. Thomas P. Brown, and left four children.
3. Jane Dinsmore[6], m. William Fletcher; no children.
4. Mary Dinsmore[6], m. Calhoun Clargston, in 1838; seven children.
5. Thomas Ross Dinsmore[6], m. Sarah Monroe, in 1834-35; two children.
6. Sarah Dinsmore[6], m. Matthew Henning, in 1844; one child, d. young.

183. Elizabeth Dinsmore[5], m. William Willock, of Pittsburg, Penn., where they lived and died, leaving

CHILDREN.

1. Nancy Willock[6], m. Richard Hope, and left six children.
2. Mary Willock[6]; single; Allegheny, Penn.
3. Sarah Ann Willock[6], m. Net Metyar, a merchant; res. Allegheny City, Penn. No children.
4. William Foster Willock[6]; merchant; d. unmarried.
5. Jane Willock[6], m. Moses Ward; six children; res. Allegheny, Penn. His son, John Scott Ward[7]; res. Allegheny, Penn.
6. John Scott Willock[6], m. Miss Hayes; res. Allegheny, Penn. Children: James Willock[7], is a banker; Lillie Willock[7]; William Willock[7], dec., was a banker; Frank Willock[7].
7. James Willock[6], d. in infancy.

184. Thomas Dinsmore[5], b. 1780, in Ireland, County Donegal; m. 1812-13, Mary Gray; res. on a farm in Rich Hill, Greene Co., Penn.

CHILDREN.

1. Robert Dinsmore[6], m. Amy Dane; several children; res. Crow's Mills, Greene Co., Penn.
2. Bythinia Dinsmore[6], m. Philip Conkle; no children; res. Crow's Mills, Greene Co., Penn.
3. Nancy Scott Dinsmore[6], m. John Vanatta; several children. She m., second, Mr. Throckmorton; no children.
4. Mary Dinsmore[6], m. Benjamin Dunbin; four children.
5. Jane Elizabeth Dinsmore[6], m. James Vanatta; one child.
6. Anne Dinsmore[6], m. Milton Beabort, and had nine children, all deceased.
7. John Gray Dinsmore[6], m. Margaret Harvey; res. Crow's Mills, Greene Co., Penn.; four children: William Dinsmore[7], Mary Dinsmore[7], Benjamin Dinsmore[7], Margaret Dinsmore[7].
8. Thomas Dinsmore[6], m. Miss Elliott; several children. He m. a second and a third wife; res. West Union, Ohio Co., W. Va.
9. Henry Dinsmore[6], m. Miss McKarihan, daughter of Joseph, and left children.

185. Moses Dinsmore[5] (190), b. 1783; res. Rich Hill, Greene Co., Penn.
186. Nancy Dinsmore[5], m. 1811, James Hamilton, of Pittsburg, Penn. "He was a whitesmith." They left six children. One was a lawyer, and is deceased.

Children of Robert Dinsmore[4], by Second Marriage.

187. Martha Pollock Dinsmore[5], b. Nov. 16, 1806; m. Andrew Thompson, April, 1827. They are deceased; no children.
188. William Dinsmore[5], b. Dec. 16, 1807; m. Charlotte Ramsay, of Washington Co., Penn., March 10, 1846; res. Belmont Co., Ohio; six sons and two daughters.
189. Margaret Paden Dinsmore[5], b. Aug. 3, 1809; m. James Hope in 1827, b. 1802, d. July 14, 1880; ten children. Robert Hope[6], res. Greensboro, Westmoreland Co., Penn. The others resside in Eastern Iowa.

190. Moses Dinsmore⁵ (185), Robert⁴, —— Dinsmore³, John², *Laird* Dinsmoor¹. He was b. in County Donegal, Ireland, in 1783, in the home on the Foyle River, three miles from the City of Londonderry, Ireland. From a child he was studious and religiously inclined, and early united with the Presbyterian Church. In 1812 he purchased a tract of land of two hundred acres in Rich Hill, Greene Co., Penn., and commenced his farm. He m. June 9, 1814, Irenæa, daughter of Francis and Elizabeth (Martin) Braddock, who was b. Sept. 20, 1790, and whose parents, about the time of the Revolution, settled in the forest of Western Pennsylvania. Mr. Dinsmore was an elder in the church. His life was one of usefulness, and he d. April 3, 1836, in his fifty-third year. Mrs. Dinsmore d. Aug. 20, 1834.

CHILDREN, BORN ON DINSMORE FARM, RICH HILL, GREENE CO., PENN.

191. Rev. Robert Scott Dinsmore⁶, b. Nov. 14, 1815; m. May 4, 1837, Margaret Loughbridge, who d. June 13, 1838; one child. He m. second in 1849, Sarah Whitham. He went that year to Iowa as a Home Missionary, and was pastor of the Presbyterian Church of Washington, Iowa, from 1849 to 1853; d. Aug. 27, 1853.

CHILDREN.

1. William Loughbridge Dinsmore⁷, b. on the Dinsmore farm, Rich Hill, Greene Co., Penn., March 13, 1838; m. in 1860, Sarah C. Wirick, b. Dec. 24, 1842. They res. Adair, Adair Co., Iowa. Children: Robert Scott Dinsmore⁸, b. Sept. 1, 1862; m. Nov. 27, 1890, at Otfumwa, Iowa. Sadie Ray Bell, b. Sept. 10, 1869. He is a carpenter and bridge builder; res. Ottumwa, Iowa. Margaret Elizabeth Dinsmore⁸, b. April 13, 1864; m. Dec. 26, 1880, Elton Booth; res. Adair, Adair Co., Iowa. William Henry Dinsmore⁷, b. Jan. 29, 1871; teacher; res. Adair, Iowa.
2. John Milton Dinsmore⁷, b. May 5, 1850; d. March 13, 1852.
3. Elizabeth Dinsmore⁷, b. 1852; res. Battle Creek, Mich.

192. Rev. Francis Braddock Dinsmore⁶, b. April 22, 1817; m. June 6, 1847, Jane Patterson, b. April 10, 1820, in Washington Co., Penn. That year he went to Iowa as a Home Missionary, and was pastor of the church at Mount Pleasant, Iowa. Two children, a son and a daughter, died in infancy.

CHILDREN.

1. William Patterson Dinsmore⁷, b. July 28, 1851; d. Aug. 15, 1853.
2. Frances Katherine Dinsmore⁷, b. at Morning Sun, Iowa, May 3, 1855; m. Henry Griffin, Jan. 25, 1877; res. Gaynor City, Mo.; five children, born at Nodaway Co., Mo.: John Monroe Griffin⁸, b. Dec. 26, 1877. Ada Jane Griffin⁸, b. June 3, 1880. Charles Walter Griffin⁸, b. Oct. 6, 1882. Lizzie Myrtle Griffin⁸, b. April 24, 1887. Ora Gertrude Griffin⁸, b. Nov. 22, 1888; d. Oct. 14, 1889.
3. John McCluskey Dinsmore⁷, b. Morning Sun, Iowa, Aug. 3, 1856; m. Cornelia E. Bucks, May 16, 1883; res. Gaynor City, Mo. Two children: Grover Cleveland Dinsmore⁸, b. Dec. 18, 1885. May Mabel Dinsmore⁸, b. July 27, 1887.

4. William Henry Dinsmore[7], b. Morning Sun, Iowa, Nov. 17, 1858; m. in Maryville, Mo., Frances T. Simmons, Sept. 8, 1886. Two children: Francis B. Dinsmore[8], b. Aug. 18, 1887. Bessie Jane Dinsmore[8], b. Dec. 3, 1888.
5. Thomas Chalmers Dinsmore[7], b. Mount Pleasant, Iowa, July 29, 1861; m. Mattie Sylva Forshee, Jan. 1, 1891; res. Gaynor City, Nodaway Co., Mo.

193. Rev. Thomas Hughes Dinsmore[6], D. D., b. Aug. 15, 1819; m. Sept. 14, 1847, Elizabeth McConaughey, b. April 13, 1822, only daughter of Robert and Mary (Anderson) McConaughey, who came from the North of Ireland. Mr. Dinsmore was a Home Missionary in Iowa. Many years were spent by him in pioneer educational work as well as in missionary labor, in Iowa, Missouri, and Kansas. His home for many years has been at Highland, Doniphan Co., Kan., where his wife died July 24, 1874.

CHILDREN.

1. Mary E. M. Dinsmore[7], b. Sept. 18, 1848; d. July 14, 1849.
2. Virginia McCheyne Dinsmore[7], b. Nov. 22, 1849; unmarried; res. Highland, Kan.
3. Archibald Alexander Dinsmore[7], b. Oct. 30, 1851; m. 1877, Lizzie Dreher, daughter of Hon. Samuel Dreher, of Stroudsburg, Penn. He is an attorney; was admitted to the bar in 1876; res. Philadelphia, Penn. Children: Bessie Dinsmore[8], b. July 1, 1878; Francis William Dinsmore[8], b. Jan. 29, 1880.
4. Robert Scott Dinsmore[7], M. D., b. Dec. 4, 1853; m. Nov. 21, 1883, Esther, daughter of Judge Wilkinson, of Troy, Kan., b. Jan. 19, 1864. Child: Bertha Dinsmore[8], b. Sept. 21, 1884; res. Troy, Doniphan Co., Kan.
5. Prof. Thomas Hughes Dinsmore[7], Jr., Ph. D., b. May 18, 1855; is professor of chemistry and physics in the State Normal School at Emporia, Kan.; res. Emporia, Kan. He m. Minnie Curtiss, daughter of Rev. Mr. Curtiss, of Preble, N. Y.
6. Francis William Dinsmore[7], b. April 21, 1857; merchant; m. Emma Adelia Toner, a teacher, June 10, 1886; res. Fairbury, Neb. Children: Archibald Hughes Dinsmore[8], b. July 25, 1887; Francis Elmer Dinsmore[8], b. Jan. 10, 1890.
7. Mary Irenæa Dinsmore[7], b. Jan. 23, 1859. She was a professor in Hastings College, Hastings, Adams Co., Neb., from 1883 to 1889. She m. Aug. 26, 1889, Daniel Upton, Jr., b. Sept. 26, 1853; bookkeeper; res. Muskegon, Mich. Child: Thomas Dinsmore Upton[8], b. Oct. 18, 1890.
8. Elizabeth McConaughey Dinsmore[7], b. March 10, 1862; unmarried; res. Highland, Kan.

194. Rev. John Martin Dinsmore[6], b. May 25, 1821; m. Martha Jane Grey, July 19, 1847, b. Feb. 19, 1826; res. Carthage, Jasper Co., Mo.

CHILDREN.

1. Mary Irenæa Dinsmore[7], b. Sept. 13, 1849; single; res. Carthage, Mo.
2. John Grey Dinsmore[7], b. Oct. 21, 1851; m. Nancy Jane Moody, Sept. 8, 1872.

CHILDREN.

I. Jessie M. Dinsmore[8], b. July 28, 1873.
II. Elmer G. Dinsmore[8], b. Dec. 5, 1875.
III. Scott Dinsmore[8], b. July 6, 1878.
IV. Roy Dinsmore[8], b. Nov. 1, 1880.
V. Kate M. Dinsmore[8], b. April 14, 1882.
VI. John Dinsmore[8], b. March 6, 1885.
VII. Joe Dinsmore[8], b. Aug. 19, 1887.

3. Martha Jane Dinsmore[7], b. Nov. 24, 1853; m. Burgen H. Brown, April 24. 1877; res. Carthage, Mo. Children: Elmer B. Brown[8], b. March 1, 1878; Clara E. Brown[8], b. April 28, 1880; Berenice S. Brown[8], b. Jan. 5, 1883; Martha J. Brown[8], b. June 7, 1885; Homer Brown[8], b. March 13, 1887.
• 4. William S. P. Dinsmore[7], b. Sept. 9, 1856; d. April 9, 1857.
5. M. Josephine Dinsmore[7], b. March 2, 1858; m. Charles Ransom, March 14, 1888.
6. Plummer L. Dinsmore[7], b. Aug. 7, 1860; m. Esther Y. Hood, June 10, 1885; he d. Sept. 6, 1886. Child: Marguerite H. Dinsmore[8], b. April 27, 1886; res. Carthage, Mo.
7. Nannie A. Dinsmore[7], b. Oct. 10, 1863; single; res. Carthage, Mo.
8. Minnie F. Dinsmore[7], b. Sept. 30, 1866; m. Ambrose E. Findley, Dec. 4, 1889; res. Springfield, Mo.

195. Elizabeth Jane Dinsmore[6], b. June 7, 1824; d. Aug. 13, 1834.
196. Nancy Anne Dinsmore[6], b. July 1, 1826; m. 1850, Hon. William H. Fitzpatrick, who d. Aug. 14, 1890. He served several terms in the Legislature of Kansas as representative and senator; res. Topeka, Kan., where his widow now resides.

CHILDREN.

1. Thomas Dinsmore Fitzpatrick[7], res. Salina, Kan.
2. Margaret Irenæa Fitzpatrick[7], res. Topeka, Kan.
3. Robert Ford Fitzpatrick[7], res. Arkansas City, Kan.
4. William Fitzpatrick[7], res. New Mexico.
5. John Scott Fitzpatrick[7], res. on the home farm, at Topeka, Kan.
6. Mary Fitzpatrick[7], res. Topeka, Kan.

197. Bathsheba Dinsmore[6], b. April 9, 1828; teacher; d. Sept. 14, 1851.
198. Moses Garvine Dinsmore[6], b. Feb. 7, 1831. He was a teacher and student, and d. when a young man, at the home of his brother, Rev. Thomas Hughes Dinsmore[6], at Washington, Iowa, Aug. 31, 1854.
199. Rev. William Henry Dinsmore[6], b. May 31, 1833; m. Lizzie Crosset, who d. May 12, 1865. He m., second, Phebe Harris, of Phillipsburg, N. J., on Sept. 16, 1867. He was pastor of the Presbyterian Church of Deerfield, N. J., and d. May 26, 1877. His burial place is at Phillipsburg, N. J.

CHILDREN.

1. William Harris Dinsmore[7], b. May 12, 1868; res. Phillipsburg, N. J.
2. Benjamin Braddock Dinsmore[7], res. Phillipsburg, N. J.

DINSMORES OF MISSISSIPPI.

200. Adam Dinsmoor[1]. He was b. in Ireland, and bore the same Christian name as one (No. 6) of the four sons of John Dinsmoor[2], the Scotch Emigrant who settled in Ballywattick, Ballymoney, County Antrim, Ireland. By his approximate age, he was probably a grandson of one of the three (Adam[2], Robert[2], Samuel[2]) brothers who remained in Ireland. He m. Miss Jackson.

CHILDREN.

201. David Dinsmore[2].
202. Samuel Dinsmore[2].
203. James Dinsmore[2] (205). m. Miss McDonald.
204. Elizabeth Dinsmore[2], m. Archibald McDonald.

205. James Dinsmore[2] (203), Adam[1]. He came from Ireland; m. Miss McDonald, and he lived in the South.

AMONG HIS CHILDREN WERE:

206. James J. Dinsmore[3], res. at or near Falkville, North Alabama, and has a family.
207. Nancy Dinsmore[3], m. Mr. Wall; res. Avoca, Ala.
208. Andrew McDonald Dinsmore[3] (209), b. 1808; res. Noxubee Co., Miss.

209. Andrew McDonald Dinsmore[3] (208), James[2], Adam[1]. He was b. April, 1808. Removed to Noxubee Co., Miss., about 1846, from North Alabama. He m. Minerva Barton Beauchamp, who d. March, 1888, in that state. He is still living, in vigorous health, and is an officer in the Presbyterian Church in Macon, Miss.

CHILD.
210. James Augustus Dinsmore[4], b. Jan. 16, 1852; m.

CHILDREN.
1. Andrew McDonald Dinsmore[5].
2. Emma Dinsmore[5].
3. Gardiner S. Dinsmore[5].
4. J. A. Dinsmore[5].
5. William Dinsmore[5].

211. John Robert Dinsmore[4] (212), b. Jan. 18, 1855; res. Macon, Miss.

212. John Robert Dinsmore[4], Andrew McDonald[3], James[2], Adam[1]. He was b. near Macon, Miss., Jan. 18, 1855; graduated at Cumberland University, Lebanon, Tenn., in June, 1876, completing his course with honor, and is, in 1890, a successful lawyer in Macon, Miss. He was a candidate for nomination to the Mississippi Legislature before he was twenty-three years of age, but was defeated. He served as Mayor of Macon for six successive years, when he was succeeded by his brother-in-law, Hon. A. T. Dent. He is popular and supported by all classes. He takes an active part in politics, and is Chairman of the Executive Committee of the Fourth Mississippi Congressional District. He is conservative and firm in his views, and has the confidence of the people. He is a deacon in the Presbyterian Church of which his father has been an elder for over forty years. He is six feet and one inch in height, and weighs over two hundred and fifty pounds. He m. a, daughter of William Dent, in Dec. 1884,

CHILD.

213. Mary Witherspoon Dinsmore[5],

A VISIT TO THE OLD DINSMORE HOME IN IRELAND, JULY 9, 1889.

This brief sketch will preserve, it is hoped, for all time the place of habitation of the Dinsmore family in the Emerald Isle, which had not been located and was entirely unknown to most of the members of the family in the United States until my investigations revealed and established it.

It had been my great desire to visit the old home of the early Dinsmoors, the abode for many generations of their descendants, whose history has been here given. John Dinsmoor[2], the Scotch lad who, with cane and broad bonnet, "hied him" from Scotland to Ireland and founded the family home at Ballywattick. with his son, John Dinsmoor[3], who came to New Hampshire, were my ancestors. All the other Dinsmoors there, in their several generations, were, in different degrees of consanguinity, my relatives.

Business of another nature called me to Ballymoney, and so I gladly embraced the opportunity of visiting one of its town-lands, Ballywattick, two miles away. With Mr. William Hunter, an occupant of part of a Dinsmoor homestead, I had enjoyed a pleasant correspondence for several years. An Irish jaunting-car, on the afternoon of the day of my arrival, bore me rapidly over the smooth, hard road to the home of Mr. Hunter, where he. his amiable wife and interesting family, gave me the cheeriest welcome. There I passed the night. They live pleasantly and cosily in a well constructed, good-sized stone house, built upon a portion of the homestead of Robert Dinsmore[4], the writer of the historic letter of 1794.

The day was misty, rainy, chilly. An open fire glowed brightly upon the hearthstones. A canary bird, forgetting its prison bars and not to be outdone in evidences of hospitality, poured forth its welcome in sharp. sweet. notes. of song. Through the windows I looked forth upon fields familiar to, and trodden by, my ancestors two hundred and more years ago, and which had been sacred to their descendants almost to the present year. A lane, lined on either side with hedges, led us to the former home of

Robert Dinsmore[4], the letter writer. It is a stone house of comfortable size and dimensions, with a roof of thatch. In its day it was one of the most pretentious in the neighborhood. It is now unoccupied. Here it was that Robert Dinsmore lived, at seventy-four years of age, in 1794, when he wrote his letter, since famous, and now historic, to his relative, John Dinsmoor, of Windham, N. II. (see p. 10), giving the genealogy and early history of the family.

That venerable man little knew the boon he was conferring upon all of his lineage who were to succeed him, by the knowledge which he imparted in that epistle. He never dreamed that his letter would become historic, and that *he* was the earliest historian of his family, and had made possible the tracing of the annals of his race into the dim past. He little thought that a century later distant kinsmen "from beyond seas" would seek out the old home, and his abode, as the place where lived a benefactor. Yet such was to be the case.

His house stands alone. The fires have gone out upon its ancient hearthstones. The calm faces of parents, disciplined and strengthened by life's cares, sufferings, and toils; the joyous ones of children, with laughing, gleeful eyes, which once appeared at those windows, are no longer there. All are gone, and forever! An air of desolation, forsakenness, and gloom prevades the ancient home and its immediate surroundings. The beating storms, the buffeting winds and tempests, shall assail no more forever the Dinsmores at that old homestead!

> Never again will the old days come.
> . . . .
> Memories? Fold them up —
> Lay them sacred by;
> What avails it to dream of the past?

The home of Samuel Dinsmore[5] (son of Robert, the letter writer) and of his son, John Dinsmore[6], now of Bloomington, Ind., was only a few rods away. William Dinsmore, called "Gentle Willie," a relative, lived close at hand, and his home is occupied by William Knox. The buildings are all of stone, very comfortable, and surrounded by tall and shapely trees, which furnish abundant shade. A lane, hedge lined, leads through pleasant fields from highway to highway. The fields are well cultivated, the country attractive and inviting to the view. A general look of thriftiness and good cheer prevails. The roads, like most of those in Great Britain, are excellent, hard and very smooth. I bade farewell to the first home of the Dinsmores in Ireland and went to Ballymoney. In the cemetery there is their quiet place of rest. There were the graves of Robert Dinsmore[4], the letter writer, of Samuel[5], his son, of Andrew[5] and William Dinsmore[5].

I took a hurried view of the small, yet historic, town where had lived another of my ancestors, Justice James McKeen, who emigrated to Londonderry, N. H., in 1719. The emigrating sons and daughters, and their descendants, of the little moorland town of Ballymoney have had a wide influence in the Scotch-American settlements in the United States.

MOTTO OF THE DINSMORE FAMILY.

The alleged motto of the Dinsmore Family is expressive and suggestive: "Spes Anchora Tuta." A free translation is: "Hope is a safe anchor."

Facts relating to Emigration to Londonderry, N. H., in 1719, wherein Mention is made of the first Scotch Settlers there and some of their Descendants.

STATEMENT OF ELIZABETH DINSMOOR[6],

William[5], Robert[4], John[3], John[2], *Laird* Dinsmoor[1]. She was a sister of the elder Governor Samuel Dinsmoor[6], of New Hampshire. She was b. in Windham, N. H., December, 1778; m. in 1801, Samuel Thom, of Windham, N. H.; removed to Denmark, Iowa, where she d. Jan. 17, 1868, aged ninety years. Her mental powers were excellent, and she delighted in reading and writing. She left numerous articles in manuscript. Her grandmother was Janet McKeen, a daughter of Justice James McKeen, of Londonderry, N. H., who came, when young,

with her father's family from Ireland, married Emigrant
John Cochran, and lived in Windham, N. H. In her old
age she recounted the incidents of the emigration to her
granddaughter, Elizabeth Dinsmore[6], about 1785, who
was not then ten years of age. It made a vivid impres-
sion on the mind of her youthful listener, who wrote out
the account, which is preserved among her manuscripts,
now in the possession of *her* great-granddaughter, Mrs.
Eliza T. Fox, of Seneca, Kan. Thus, after one hundred
and seventy-two years since the emigration, this account,
never before in print, is presented to the public.

Mrs. Elizabeth (Dinsmore[6]) Thom says: "My grandmother was nearly half a day relating the circumstances
of their emigration and settlement in this country. I was
between seven and eight years old at the time, and lis-
tened with deep interest to her narrative. My grandmother said she was a native of the North of Ireland,
which was settled from Scotland. Her forefathers were
among the first who renounced Popery, and were much
persecuted by the Catholics. Her father, James McKeen,
resolved to emigrate to America, where he could peace-
fully enjoy the religion of his choice. Having disposed
of his property, he embarked with his preacher, Rev.
James McGregor, and sixteen others, who had bound
themselves to him for a certain time to pay for their
passage to America.

"It was Sunday when they reached Boston, and the
pious emigrants celebrated the joyful occasion by singing
psalms of praise to that God who had brought them in
safety to the shores of the New World. Their fervent
piety secured them a warm reception among the inhabi-
tants of Boston, but after a brief stay at that place, they
hired hunters to guide them through the wilderness to
Beaver Pond, in Nutfield, afterward called Londonderry. There they pitched their tents and had religious
services. My grandmother, though only ten years old at
that time, could remember the text and much of the dis-
course. Her memory was excellent, and she had the deep
religious feeling of the Puritans of those times."

The fact that James McKeen, who was a man of means,
had advanced the passage money for his neighbors and

kinsmen who were less successful than himself, to my knowledge, has never before been promulgated, and as it was his own daughter who made the statement, herself an emigrant, and familiar with all the circumstances of the emigration — it is not to be questioned.

The first sixteen settlers (with their families) of Londonderry, N. H., were all of Scotch blood. They were as follows: James McKeen, John Barnet, Archibald Clendenin, John Mitchell, James Starrett, James Anderson, Randall Alexander, James Gregg, James Clark, James Nesmith, Allen Anderson, Robert Weir, John Morison, Samuel Allison, Thomas Steele, John Stuart. According to Parker's History of Londonderry, N. H., "James McKeen was one of the principal originators of the enterprise" and was "the patriarch of the colony."

The relationship between those early settlers was very near, and their intimacy of the closest kind, as will be seen from the following facts: Among them James McKeen had one, and probably two brothers-in-law, with their families. His first wife was Janet Cochran, and his daughter, Janet, m. John Cochran, of Windham, N. H. Another daughter, Elizabeth, m. James Nesmith, in Ireland, who was one of the famous sixteen settlers. Mr. McKeen lived at one time in Ballymoney, County Antrim, Ireland, only two miles from the homes of the Dinsmoors, with whom he must have been acquainted.

In Ireland Mr. McKeen m. second, Annis Cargil. Rev. James McGregor, of Aghadowey, County of Londonderry, Ireland, m. her sister, Marion Cargil, and came to Londonderry, N. H., and was the first minister there.

Capt. James Gregg, one of the sixteen settlers, m. Janet Cargil, probably a sister of the others. Thomas Steele m. in Ireland, Martha Morison, a sister of John Morison, which made those two brothers-in-law. Samuel Allison m. in Ireland, Katherine Steele, a supposed sister of Thomas Steele, which linked them together. Two others of the sixteen, Allen and James Anderson, were brothers.

Rev. James McGregor, and most, if not all, of the sixteen first emigrants, were from the parish of Aghadowey, County of Londonderry, Ireland, a description and brief history of which has already been given. (See pp. 25–36.)

James Morison, a brother of John, and my ancestor; Robert Armstrong, ancestor of the Armstrongs of Windham, N. H., and of George W. Armstrong, Esq., a prominent business gentleman of Boston, Mass.; and John Bell,—quickly joined the colony mentioned before. According to a family tradition, which is accepted as truth, the earliest known ancestor of the Bells of New Hampshire was Matthew Bell, who was born at Kirk Connell, in Scotland. (There are seven places of this name in Scotland, and no identification has been made.) His son, John Bell, was born in Ballymoney, County of Antrim, Ireland, in 1678; m. Elizabeth, daughter of John and Rachel (Nelson) Todd; came to Londonderry, N. H., in 1720, where he died July 8, 1743, leaving a numerous posterity.

This work will close with a poem of rare merit, which is particularly appropriate, as it relates to Scotch, or Scotch-Irish, achievement, suffering, long endurance amid famine, pestilence, and death, and final glorious triumph. The ancestors of many who read this volume were on the side of William, in the famous struggle between James the Second and William, Prince of Orange, for the English throne. Many of them were in the besieged City of Londonderry, Ireland, endured the horrors, witnessed and were thrilled with the great joy of final victory, all of which the great English historian, Macaulay, describes with graphic power in his History of England. The author of this poem has, with rare power, depicted the "City of the Foyle," as it was and as it remains to-day. The main events of the celebrated siege, when the gates of the city were closed in the face of an insolent foe by a band of noble "Apprentice Boys"; the fierce attacks of the enemy, the bursting of the boom which the foe had stretched across the Foyle to prevent ships loaded with provisions from succoring the starving city, are rehearsed in an elevated and spirited manner. The writer is a descendant of Capt. James Gregg, who was born in Ayrshire, Scotland, and, with his parents, went to Ireland about 1690, and was one of the first sixteen settlers of Londonderry, N. H., in 1719, as previously stated.

Although the author of the poem never visited Londonderry, Ireland, never trod its "steep, ascending streets," never saw its "sacred walls," worshipped in "the old cathedral on the heights," nor bathed her hands in the flowing waters of the Foyle, yet her description of the city and all within it, as well as its surroundings, are wonderfully accurate, — they are almost without a flaw. The poem is inserted with the hope that it may afford my readers as much pleasure and joy as it has given me.

THE HEROES OF THE SIEGE OF LONDONDERRY, IRELAND, 1688-89.

BY MISS LUCINDA JANE GREGG, OF DERRY, N. H.

There 's many a prouder citadel, there 's many a grander town,
Among the thousand battle-fields on which the stars look down;
But never place held hero hearts more resolute and strong
Than brave old Londonderry, famed in story and in song.

Hill of the Oaks! we see, unchanged, thy sacred walls arise:
Still up thy steep, ascending streets the ancient pathway lies;
Still at thy foot the river flows with broad, majestic sweep,
And still the grand cathedral crowns thy narrow summit steep.

No rock of stern Gibraltar lifts its dark, defiant wall;
No fortress rises from the sea to shield thy towers tall;
More glorious far than rock or fort built up by time or toil,
The Rock of Ages is thy trust, brave City of the Foyle!

Flow on, historic river, sing the story of the free;
Repeat it proudly to the sky — go tell it to the sea!
Send far, O sea! the thrilling song across Atlantic's wave,
And bid these echoing hills send back the anthem of the brave.

The haughty foe came boldly up with weapons keen and bright;
Within those narrow walls each face paled quickly at the sight;
One startling cry rang wildly up from street to palace dome, —
"The gates! the gates! close fast the gates! For freedom and our
    home!"

Loud called a band of hero lads, all resolute and bold,
"Quick to the guard house! Seize the keys away from traitor's hold!"
Down to the water gate they rushed where rolled the river low,
And quickly drew the drawbridge up in face of all the foe!

The heavy gates swung grandly round, in triumph, one by one;
The great key turned the massive bolt,—the glorious deed was done!
Glad Freedom walked the hillside streets and saw, adown the land,
The army of a king defied by that heroic band.

Courageous citadel! thy fate is told with faltering breath;
Full well those bold defenders knew 't was victory or death!
They looked their narrow fortress o'er, reviewed their few strong men,
Opened their scanty magazine, and pledged each other then.

One earnest prayer to Heaven they sent, one firm resolve they made,
Then bound the white badge on their arms while burst the cannonade;
That sacred badge would lead them on to conquer or to die,
For "No surrender" thrilled each heart and flashed from every eye.

Then burst the dreadful shot and shell, and fast the fire came down;
The roaring of the culverin resounded through the town;
The river blazed with lightning, and the red-hot cannon balls
Thundered against the trembling gates and shook the dark old walls.

The tumult and the terror of War's horrible alarms
With deep and dreadful anguish filled that citadel in arms;
Yet still that glorious badge they wore through every fearful hour,—
Still waved the crimson banner from the high cathedral tower.

Upon that crowded garrison the summer's sun shone down,
And dread disease came through the gates with fearful, fatal frown;
Then frightful famine leaped the walls and shook his spectral shield,
And deadly foes all joined to make the faithful fortress yield.

Ah! hushed was every hillside home, and stilled was every song,
As paled the famished faces of that starving, suffering throng;
Wan skeletons with trembling steps the battered bulwarks trod,
And thousands, ere the summer waned, lay dead beneath the sod.

Their holy altars and their homes,—for these they perilled all;
And still the banner waved on high, still stood the firm old wall;
Still "No surrender" thrilled each heart and nerved each dying hand,
And every home was hallowed by the heroism grand!

The old cathedral on the heights knew well their wants and woes;
There, pleading prayers ascended oft, sweet sounds of peace arose,
While from the roof the sounds of war went booming loud and long;
There blazed the beacon light that told the peril of the throng.

One startling sound was echoed from the river to the rock!
"The ships! the ships are coming! yes, the fleet is in the Lough!"
All eagerly the famished crowd climbed up the fortress wall,
And saw upon the happy tide the vessels rise and fall.

Life! life was in the swelling sails and in the blissful breeze;
Too weak, too faint for rapturous cheers, they dropped upon their
    knees;
Tears of thanksgiving told their joy, but never shout or song,—
Ah! God had heard the faithful prayers of that heroic throng.

The bold besiegers on the shore their batteries opened wide;
Against the ships the blazing balls came thundering o'er the tide;
The starving crowd upon the walls saw life's last hope assailed,
But God was with those gallant ships, and safely on they sailed.

Wild rose the joy — when suddenly one vessel ran aground!
"The boom! the boom!" and shouting foes the perilled ship came
    round;
"Oh! now or never!" was the cry that rose from livid lips
And hearts of agony that watched the struggle of the ships.

All petrified with silent grief, amid the fearful strife,
They saw go down the trembling tide their last dear hope of life;
But God was with those heroes still — the glorious ship sent back
A sudden, fearful, fiery charge across the foaming track.

One quick rebound, and she was safe! the ships were seen to ride,
Amid the yells of furious foes, triumphant o'er the tide!
Right onward toward the joyful town the conquering vessels passed;
'T was life! sweet life! 't was home! dear home! 't was victory at last!

Index of Dinsmoors-Dinsmores, and Others.

www.ingramcontent.com/pod-product-compliance
Lightning Source LLC
Chambersburg PA
CBHW031814090426
42739CB00008B/1269